The Sunday After

Preaching in Moments and Movements

Clarence E. Wright
Foreword by Marvin A. McMickle

T0270236

JUDSON PRESS
PUBLISHERS SINCE 1824
VALLEY FORGE, PA

The Sunday After: Preaching in Moments and Movements
© 2022 by Judson Press, Valley Forge, PA 19482-0851
All rights reserved.

Judson Press has made every effort to trace the ownership of all quotes. In the event of a question arising from the use of a quote, we regret any error made and will be pleased to make the necessary correction in future printings and editions of this book.

Bible quotations in this volume are from *The Holy Bible*, King James Version; HOLY BIBLE, New International Version®, NIV®, copyright © 1973, 1978, 1984, 2011 by Biblica Inc. Used by permission. All rights reserved worldwide; New Revised Standard Version of the Bible, copyright © 1989 by the Division of Christian Education of the National Council of the Churches of Christ in the United States of America. Used by permission. All rights reserved.

And from the New Revised Standard Version of the Bible, copyright © 1989 by the Division of Christian Education of the National Council of the Churches of Christ in the United States of America. Used by permission. All rights reserved.

Interior design by Wendy Ronga, Hampton Design Group.
Cover design by Lisa Delgado, Delgado and Company.

Library of Congress Cataloging-in-Publication data

Cataloging-in-Publication Data available upon request. Contact cip@judson-press.com.

Printed in the U.S.A.
First printing, 2022.

Contents

Foreword

Harry Emerson Fosdick, one of the great preachers of the 20th century, offered an insight into the content of sermons that every preacher should consider. He said, "Only the preacher proceeds upon the idea that folk come to church desperately anxious to discover what happened to the Jebusites."[1] The truth is, people come to church anxious to hear a message that is rooted in scripture, applicable to their own lives, and capable of shedding light upon the circumstances that surround them every day. That is especially the case when some significant event has occurred in their local community, in the country where they live, or on the global stage. When something like that happens, people come to church hoping to hear something that puts those intrusive events into perspective.

I learned this lesson through hard experience. I was scheduled to preach on September 17, 2001, and my sermon for that Sunday was already announced and ready to be preached. However, on September 11, 2001, there were three terrorist attacks on the United States. One took place in New York City where two jet airliners intentionally crashed into the World Trade Center. Another took place in Washington, DC, where another plane intentionally crashed into the Pentagon. The third terrorist attack was thwarted when the plane that was heading for either the US Capitol or the White House was brought down when the passengers on that flight rushed the terrorists that had seized control of that plane and caused that plane to crash in an open field in Shanksville, PA.

It was immediately apparent to me that the text and topic I had planned for the Sunday after September 11, 2001, was not what anyone in my congregation in Cleveland, OH, wanted to hear. The third plane, the one that crashed in Pennsylvania, was scheduled to fly to California. However, we knew by the end of the day that the California-bound plane made its turn to Washington, DC, right over our heads in the skies above Cleveland. No sermon on stewardship, discipleship, or heavenly citizenship would have been well received on the Sunday after September 11. My planned sermon had to be set aside. The fears and anxieties of the congregation brought on by those terrorist attacks took precedence over my planned sermon. As the German-born theologian, Paul Tillich said, "Preaching must be done with an awareness of the present moment."[2] On the Sunday after a terrorist attack on the United States, most preachers knew they had to address the present moment!

What preachers had to figure out on their own in 2001 remains the same more than twenty years later. Whether the issue is the death of George Floyd, the domestic terrorist attack on the nation's Capitol, the destruction caused by a weather-related event, or the death of a significant leader on the national stage, a good preacher knows he or she must speak to such a major event, because such an event has already captured the attention of those seated in the congregation, listening by TV, or watching the livestream. The difference between now and then is the availability of a book that can challenge and equip preachers today on how they can effectively embrace the need to preach on the Sunday after such major events have occurred.

Clarence Wright has produced such a book in *The Sunday After: Preaching in Moments and Movements*. This book reminds preachers that their sermon schedule needs to be sufficiently adaptable so they can quickly adjust to speak about things happening in the present moment. As Wright points out, that adaptability might require a last-minute change in text and topic. He says in this book, "Sermons written on Saturday night are sometimes necessitated by the events of Saturday evening." In other words, whatever has already been written and rehearsed for the next morning may need to be set aside because of some major event whose importance cannot be ignored.

To demonstrate how this can be done, Wright takes two separate approaches. First, he focuses on the way that various professors of preaching discuss the importance of preaching about current events. In doing so, he looks at the work of Kenyatta Gilbert, Cleophus Larue, O. Wesley Allen, Frank Thomas, the late Henry Mitchell, and Marvin McMickle. Each of them offers a biblical and theological rationale for why preaching about significant current events is an essential part of a preacher's responsibility.

Then Wright turns from the theoretical and academic to the practical. He examines several sermons that were preached in response to such a major social event, namely the death of Trayvon Martin and the not guilty verdict awarded to George Zimmerman, an event that shocked many African Americans to their core. Wright selected sermons from Leslie Callahan, Howard John Wesley, Renita Weems, Otis Moss III, Prathia Hall, and Roger Ray. He then offers one of his own sermons so the reader of this book can see how Wright made this adjustment himself on the Sunday after.

One of the key insights in this book is that preachers need to learn from writers how to address major current events. Wright reminds his readers that persons like James Baldwin, Ta Nahisi Coates, Howard Thurman, and James Cone have managed to use their platforms as writers to bring such major issues into focus in the present moment. One could add other names to that list including Cornel West, Michael Eric Dyson, Isabel Wilkerson, and Toni Morrison. What none of those persons ever had to do, however, was preach to the same congregation Sunday after Sunday, and decide when and how to shift away from a pre-planned sermon to preach (not write) about a major event that burst its way into the news and into the anxious minds of a waiting congregation. That is what preaching on the Sunday after is all about.

The first time I encountered Clarence Wright's idea about preaching after some major event had occurred, he was my student at Colgate Rochester Crozer Divinity School. This book began as a Doctor of Ministry project, which he diligently prepared and confidently defended before a faculty committee. When I reviewed this book manuscript two years later, it had evolved from the doctoral work of a student to the scholarly work of a peer that is deserving of the attention of preachers and professors of preaching as they do their work "with an awareness of the present moment." This book is not about the ancient Jebusites. This book is about how to preach after COVID has disrupted our lives, after Donald Trump and his MAGA movement have all but destroyed our democratic institutions, and after one unarmed Black person after another has been shot and killed by white police officers or self-appointed vigilantes. This book will help preachers on what to say on the Sunday After such events occur.

In our last class together, I shared with Clarence Wright and five or six other students the story of how Dr. Gardner Taylor once showed me a great kindness in 1971 by giving $10 to me and three other students from Union Theological Seminary in New York City. He gave each of us $10 so we could buy a meal one Sunday evening, knowing that Union did not serve meals on the weekend. Dr. Taylor said that he did not want or expect us to return to Concord Baptist Church in Brooklyn, NY, to repay him for his generosity. Instead, he wanted us to pass that $10 on to others "every chance we got for as long as we lived." I have always viewed my interactions with younger preachers and seminary students as a way to pay forward the $10 given to me so long ago. I challenged the students in that class at CRCDS to take the lessons they learned from me and pass them on every chance they get or as long as they live. The students in that class now call themselves "the $10 crew." Clarence Wright is a member of that $10 crew, and he is paying forward his $10 in this timely book. I could not be prouder of him as he seeks to empower the preaching and the preachers of this current generation, making them aware of the present moment.

Rev. Marvin A. McMickle, DMin and PhD
Retired President of Colgate Rochester Crozer Divinity School,
Rochester, New York
Pastor Emeritus of Antioch Baptist Church in Cleveland, Ohio

Notes

1. "Lessons in Preaching from Harry Emerson Fosdick," ministrymagazine.org, June 2019.

2. Paul Tillich quoted in *The Preaching of the Gospel* by Karl Barth (Philadelphia, PA: Westminster Press, 1963, 54).

Acknowledgments

I would like to acknowledge and thank the following for their role in shaping and creating this book:

To the God who called me to preach and is worth preaching about.

To my best friend and partner in life, Corinne, for love and unwavering support.

To my mom, Betty Jean Bacon, and my dad, Rev. LeRoy Glenn Wright, who raised me, invested in me, and continued to inspire me.

To my Love Zion Baptist Church family, who have watched me grow and have grown with me. Thank you for letting me practice my preaching every "Sunday After." I am truly blessed to serve as your pastor.

To Judson Press, thank you for giving a shot to a first-timer and for a legacy of quality publishing that helped form me long before I was privileged to join your ranks as an author.

To my Missio Seminary colleagues, thank you for the courage to have tough conversations and embracing what it means to truly follow Jesus into the world. I am particularly grateful to David T. Lamb, R. Todd Mangum, Frank A. James III, and Carolyn Custis James for their encouragement and collected wisdom through the proposal process.

To my alma mater Colgate Rochester Crozer Divinity School, for the environment and tools to pursue the research that became this book.

To Marvin A. McMickle, my mentor and inspiration as a preacher, scholar, and author. I am doing my part to continue your legacy of scholarship and practice and pass along my "$10."

To the "$10 crew," especially Lewis Dixon and Marco D. McNeil, my brothers for life. We hold each other accountable to pass our knowledge and experience to the world.

To Leslie D. Callahan, my model of a thinking preacher and evidence that you can be a scholar with a pastor's heart.

To Frank A. Thomas, who in one five-minute conversation in 2018 set me on the path that would become this book.

Introduction

The Sunday after Trayvon Martin was shot, I had to preach. The Sunday after Mike Brown lay lifeless on the Ferguson concrete, I had to preach. When George Floyd, Breonna Taylor, and countless others lost their lives and our cities burned with rage, there was always a Sunday after. The question *what shall I preach?* is constant for those called to deliver God's word, but the weight of that moment is even more pronounced when following high-profile incidents of racial injustice. From the perspective of the pulpit, this book addresses this relevant topic with the backdrop of what the *New York Times* described as "the largest civil rights movement in U.S. history."[1] A healthy perspective on the intersection of current events and Christian faith is crucial for effective ministry, whether racial tensions, a world-changing pandemic, record local violence in urban communities, or extreme political polarization, all of which have marked recent years. What lies in the pages ahead seeks to fill a glaring need for pastors and spiritual care providers because there is no shortage of moments to address, and Sunday is always coming.

People hold competing ideologies about how the preaching of the gospel should relate to current events in contemporary society. Some view current events as a distraction that should have no bearing on the presentation of the gospel, while others view the use of current events as essential to keep sermons relevant in a changing world. Some believe that the gospel of salvation through Jesus Christ should stand on its own without the help of pop culture or the daily news cycle, while others would characterize a gospel that does not engage current events as powerless. While certainly room for nuance exists between these two polarizing positions, this book seeks to show that engagement with current events in the preaching ministry is not only permissible and advantageous but also biblical and crucial to the effective delivery of the gospel. This has been especially true in recent years when the very public deaths of African Americans at the hands of law enforcement have been a source of communal trauma that demands attention in the sermonic moment. This book examines the theological premise and homiletic method of effective sermons preached in response to events of racial injustice as they coincide with other social and cultural shifts.

The opening chapter will lay the groundwork for the full book answering the question of whether preaching should respond to current events by addressing counterarguments, giving scriptural rationales, and relevant parallels in popular media. The remaining chapters narrow the focus to the issue of racial injustice and specific events that have precipitated sermonic responses in the Black Lives Matter (BLM) era. While the methods in this book were birthed from observing the BLM age, they are equally applicable to social movements of the past, as well as those that will surely occur in the future. Chapter 2 emphasizes hope as a guiding theology and goal of preaching when addressing events that relate to racial injustice. Chapter 3 examines relevant scholarship that addresses the risks of responsive preaching and the balance needed to effectively construct potentially controversial sermon content. Chapter 4 provides an in-depth case study centered on sermons preached on July 14, 2013, which was the Sunday after the not-guilty verdict in George Zimmerman's trial for the killing of Trayvon Martin. Chapter 5 presents a four-part homiletic strategy based on the sermons studied in chapter 4. Chapter 6 demonstrates how that road map was applied on Sunday, May 31, 2020, which followed the death of George Floyd at the hands of officer Derek Chauvin in Minneapolis, and the international protests that followed. Together these events and the corresponding "Sunday after" represent two of the significant milestones in the BLM movement. The conclusion highlights the importance of maintaining the celebratory nature of Black preaching as an act of resistance.

While the contents of this book are largely based on my doctoral research, this is not merely an academic text for theorists to ponder. I am first and foremost a practitioner. While I am a professor of homiletics, my practice as a local church pastor has informed this work and is what will prayerfully make it helpful to others who like me wrestle with these issues every Sunday. My ministry context has been the Love Zion Baptist Church, a multigenerational, predominantly and historically Black congregation located in urban North Philadelphia and affiliated with the Progressive National Baptist Convention. In keeping with this ministry context, sermons and relevant scholarship have been primarily (although not exclusively) selected from the greater Black church tradition, with the study of the last two hundred years of historic Black preaching with an emphasis on events of racial injustice that have directly affected Black Americans in the twenty-first century and defined the BLM era.

However, while the research and writing come from a uniquely and unapologetically Black position, the principles of effective preaching in this era are nevertheless applicable to various contexts. I encourage those of other cultures or contexts who feel like a fly on the wall reading the content of this book to press through. Incidents of racial injustice and the movement they inspire affect the whole world. Preachers of all backgrounds can benefit from thoughtful reflection on effective approaches, particularly those informed by those of us who work in the Black church and community.

Notes
1. Larry Buchanan, Quoctrung Bui, and Jugal K. Patel, "Black Lives Matter May Be the Largest Movement in U.S. History," *New York Times*, July 3, 2020, https://www.nytimes.com/interactive/2020/07/03/us/george-floyd-protests-crowd-size.html.

CHAPTER 1

To Serve This Present Age

The Necessity of Current Event Preaching

The movement that has become known as Black Lives Matter (BLM) can be traced to a series of shocking and heartbreaking moments. Trayvon Martin, Tamir Rice, Mike Brown, Sandra Bland, Breonna Taylor, and George Floyd are not merely a list of names invoked at protests—each one is attached to a tragic event that captivated public outrage and dominated the news cycle. Before we narrow our focus to specific incidents of racial injustice and the sermons they produced, let us ask: why it is necessary to address current events in sermons? While some are resistant to the task of deliberately crafting sermons that respond to events in the news cycle or popular culture, Scripture, tradition, and even secular culture give evidence of the need for effective engagement with current events.

Jesus Christ's words recorded in Luke 12 provide a scriptural basis for preaching that is responsive to current events. "He said to the crowd: 'When you see a cloud rising in the west, immediately you say, "It's going to rain," and it does. And when the south wind blows, you say, "It's going to be hot," and it is. Hypocrites! You know how to interpret the appearance of the earth and the sky. How is it that you don't know how to interpret this present time?'" (Luke 12:54-56, NIV). The notion of interpreting "this present time" is not an emerging fad or a gimmick of contemporary preachers to appear relevant. It is a mandate illustrated and demonstrated

by Jesus himself. Interpreting the present times is every bit as crucial as interpreting the biblical text itself; the two must be conduct-
ed in balance with one another. The Scriptures become dated and
irrelevant when not reconciled with the present times, and the present times become godless and chaotic when not reconciled with
Scripture. Preachers of the gospel bear the responsibility to deliver
the timeless message of the gospel in the context of our present time
(see, for example, Danielle Ayers and Reginald Williams Jr., *To
Serve This Present Age: Social Justice Ministries in the Black
Church* [Valley Forge, PA: Judson Press, 2013]). The second verse
of the classic hymn penned by Charles Wesley echoes this senti-
ment: "To serve the present age, my calling to fulfill: Oh, may it all
my powers engage to do my Master's will!"[1] The age has changed
since Wesley's eighteenth-century hymn was first sung, but our call
to serve has not. From the pre- and post-exilic prophets of the
Hebrew Bible to Jesus Christ himself in the New Testament, to
twentieth-century preachers like Martin Luther King Jr. and a host
of courageous voices today, the most effective prophetic voices in
history have been those who interpreted, engaged, and reformed
prevailing culture by responding to the events of their present
times. Despite this scriptural and historic evidence of the necessity
and effectiveness of current event preaching, some disagree with
the practice.

Arguments against Current Event Preaching

In an article entitled "Five Reasons Not to Preach About Current
Events," Andy Flowers argues against engaging current events in
sermons. The five reasons that Flowers offers are that he does not
want CNN to dictate his sermons, he does not want people to get
"politics fatigue" at church, he is not a political pundit, good sermons take time to write, and the Word of God is relevant.[2] In his
first reason for not preaching about current events, Flowers

laments the constant news cycle and endless breaking news. He states, "I don't want to talk about what the news tells me I should talk about; I want to talk about something far more important."[3] Flowers is correct that the news cycle can be overwhelming, and it is not prudent or possible to address everything that cable news deems worthy of coverage. However, it would be equally short-sighted to ignore events that directly affect the lives of the people in the congregation. The news should not dictate our regular preaching schedule, but sometimes the news should cause us to turn to God and offer the people direction through the power of Scripture.

In reference to "politics fatigue," Flowers cites declining ratings in the NFL due to anthem protests. He describes it as a "yucky feeling" to be "stirred up and outraged and divided." He states that he does not want to keep "wallowing in the worries of this world" but rather wants to be "reminded of eternal, transcendent, glorious things."[4] The problem with this line of thinking is that the gospel is limited to encouragement and hope for the future while being stripped of the power to effect positive change in the present. The power of the gospel is not in appeasing our personal desires and maintaining the comfort of our status quo. The gospel must challenge us to leave our various comfort zones and create a more just world.

Flowers claims to be a Bible pundit, not a political pundit, preferring to stick with his area of expertise, which is proclaiming the Word of God. I am struck by how he uses politics and current events interchangeably. While politics are often revealed through opinions on current events, current events are not inherently political. Current events are the context in which we find ourselves—the culture which we must address with the gospel. I also do not see evidence of the biblical prophets or Jesus being apolitical. First-century Palestine under Roman occupation was a very political environment. One could not effectively minister at that time without engaging the culture and politics. Even the basic statement

"Jesus is Lord" was inherently political. I contend that the same is true of twenty-first-century America—in a divisive political environment, a stand must be taken to uphold the principles of God.

As for the argument that good sermons take time to write, Flowers argues that because of time and prayer invested, whole sermons should not be rewritten to address the latest current event. Rather, the addition of an application point or adjusting an illustration will suffice. There are times when this is true—I admit that nothing is more frustrating than working all week on a sermon, and then something major happens on Saturday night that must be addressed. Sometimes a short statement or an extra point will do, but at other times, the event is so momentous that it requires the full sermon to be reworked. No sermon series is so important that it requires ignoring what weighs heavily on the people's hearts. The preaching of God's Word cannot be so didactic that we ignore the need for prophetic wisdom. Our hours of study are meant to enhance and make clear the revelation of God, never to outweigh it.

In his fifth and final point, Flowers argues that the Word of God is relevant in and of itself without the need to address specific current events. This notion defies the very definition of the word *relevant*, which specifically has to do with what is germane to contemporary interests in the current time. The Bible is absolutely relevant, but only when it is used to address matters of concern today. The truth of the Word is relevant. The identity of God is relevant. Jesus's teachings and the work of the Holy Spirit are all relevant, but to use the Word in all its relevant power requires us to address the actual concerns of our time rather than generically glossing over them with theological vagaries.

Benjamin Vrbicek provides more nuance on current event preaching, but like Flowers, he ultimately views the practice negatively. He presents a series of questions to determine when it is appropriate to address a current event during worship. First, he asks whether the event should be addressed during worship.

Pastors have other options including the church's weekly email or social media. If the decision is made to address it during worship, Vrbicek asks, "Should it be done between worship songs or within the announcements, pastoral prayer, or sermon?"[5] If it is addressed during the sermon, he offers additional concerns to weigh: "How much time should it get? Just a passing comment to show awareness or an in-depth analysis?"[6] Vrbicek also suggests asking, "Was the current event a national or global event, such as a hurricane, or shooting, or airplane crash . . . or is the current event a local one?"[7] He rightfully states, "These questions aren't theoretical to me. I wrestle with them 52 times a year."[8] This is true for all pastors who preach regularly; however, while we all wrestle with these questions, we come to drastically different answers.

Vrbicek expresses some valid concerns. For instance, he states, "What is said on Sundays must be absolutely true. I can walk back a tweet that was hastily thumbed into cyberspace, but great vigilance should be taken that this won't need to be done for what is said in a sermon."[9] I agree that the presentation of the gospel must be done with the highest integrity. A preacher should have a standard that is even higher than journalists when it comes to the presentation of facts. While his concerns are legitimate, I believe he misses the point of what it is to address current events in sermons. The nature and facts of the events themselves are merely a backdrop or a launching point for the preaching of the gospel. We must make every effort to ensure that we present factual current events, but the power of our sermons lies in the truth of the gospel, not the current events.

This overly cautious approach leads Vrbicek to some inaccurate assumptions about current event preaching and those who practice it. He states, "I think some people, including some pastors, love to follow current events the way a sports fan follows his or her team. For these people, staying current is a hobby. They do it because they think it's important, but also because it's fun to be in the know."[10] I take great issue with the classification of staying current as "a hobby." Contrary to Vrbicek's comment, it is not always "fun to be in the know." There are many current events I wish I did not know about and that I would certainly rather not address during Sunday service. Ignoring current events, whether locally or worldwide, is the easy way out. The challenge is to stay abreast of the current social and cultural environment while being constantly in prayer about how to address it. The notion of separation from the world to be immersed in God's Word alone as a spiritual virtue is short-sighted and ultimately harmful. Nothing is inherently holy or pietistic about ignorance. Spiritual interaction with the world that we live in is the heart of the incarnation. Jesus himself modeled the necessity to reconcile the Word of God with the issues of this world.

Vrbicek also speaks to the logistic issues of responding to current events. He says, "I'm not going to spend an hour before church every Sunday checking online to see what happened around the world while I slept. I don't have time (and I don't make time) each week before church to look at Fox, CNN, local news sources, or personal social media feeds."[11] He seems to make the same mistake that Flowers does of confusing political punditry with speaking as a prophet of God. Preaching current events is not opining about the news—it is proclaiming the hope of God to a broken world. This does not happen by watching CNN on Sunday morning. This happens by living a life that is incarnational, constantly reconciling God's Word with our present times. Vrbicek states, "When pastors major on the urgent, we can inadvertently lead people to forget that 'the word of our God will stand forever.'"[12] However, the way people know that the Word of our God will stand forever is by showing them how the Word of God stands today. When a terrorist attack or a natural disaster or a local tragedy happens, the people need to be reminded that the Word of our God stands and speaks to our current situation.

Still, as preachers, we must be careful when and how we respond to the daily news cycle. Trevin Wax offers four questions to consider before addressing a current event. First, "Is this a history-making event that demands the church's immediate response?"[13] By "history-making" Wax is referring to "events that instantly change the conversation and atmosphere for everyone in society."[14] He cites September 11 and the assassination of John F. Kennedy as examples. Of these "generation-shaping moments" he says, "To not respond to these events would fail to speak to the fears, worries, and concerns currently overwhelming the congregation."[15] I agree that this is a key question to ask, but I believe that these moments happen far more than the "generational" events that Wax refers to. Obviously, an event of that magnitude must be addressed during service, but many more impactful incidents can happen during any given week that also require spiritual guidance for the congregation.

Second, Wax asks, "How 'top of mind' or 'close at hand' is the recent cultural event?" Indeed, timing matters. Wax notes that when a major event like a terrorist attack or a natural disaster happens before service or the night before, "the congregation will be reeling from the news as they arrive at worship that morning."[16] He says, "When we decide not to address something (either through prayer or preaching) that is on nearly everyone's minds, we lose an opportunity to show how the gospel applies to all of life. We miss the opportunity to provide hope in a dark moment."[17] Providing hope in life's dark moments is the preeminent task for preachers of the gospel. Without confronting the current darkness with the gospel's hope, the preaching task becomes an academic exercise more concerned with word studies and authorial intent than the power of the Holy Spirit and God's Word to affect our current situation. The Word of God is "living and active" (Hebrews 4:12, NRSV). To maintain power, it must never be disconnected from our current reality. As such, preachers should be careful when addressing something in the moment when it is still fresh and raw. These moments require deep prayer and spiritual reflection. A major event or tragedy should always be addressed at the time in which it happens through a prayer or special statement, but there are times when a full sermon requires more time and reflection. Only guidance from the Spirit can determine which pathway is appropriate.

Third, Wax asks, "Are you in danger of leading your church to be driven by current events?"[18] With this question, Wax argues that "it is not the purpose of the gathered church to address every world tragedy or big political event. Where would one stop? In any week, news from all over the world could, in theory, swamp the service."[19] To view addressing current events as "swamping" the service, Wax is missing the point of why addressing these events is necessary. Wax says, "Worship should lift our eyes from the swirl of worldly worries to the King and kingdom that transcends the momentary cloud."[20] He makes this statement as a suggestion to avoid too frequently addressing current events, but I see this statement as a reason to address them even more. To "lift our eyes from the swirls of worldly worries to the King" requires first acknowledging the "momentary cloud" that we are in. As preachers of the gospel, we are the worship leaders who extend the rope of the gospel to elevate the church from the cares of their daily life. Without contextualization in the very real events of everyday life, our messages lack the power to transcend.

Fourth and finally, Wax asks, "Are we in a cultural moment where the church's guidance may be necessary?"[21] He views this as a judgment call. He encourages pastors deciding whether to address these moments to be clear about where their churches stand on the issues. He says that "pastors must judge wisely and carefully on matters related to their own congregation and when they sense their guidance and voice is required."[22] I agree that we each must be sensitive to our own contexts, but I also believe that giving spiritual guidance to the church during important moments in our culture is our primary task as pastors and preachers. The question that must be answered in each of our contexts is: what qualifies as a major cultural moment? This question must be asked weekly for those called upon to preach.

Preaching on current events is not the sole mandate. We must preach the gospel and view current events through the lens of the gospel. Pastor Geoff Sinibaldo notes that Swiss theologian Karl Barth is often quoted as saying, "We must hold the Bible in one hand and the newspaper in the other."[23] However, Sinibaldo clarifies that Barth said, "Take your Bible and take your newspaper, and read both. But interpret newspapers from your Bible."[24] The more accurate quotation maintains the authority of Scripture to guide our theology while emphasizing the need to stay abreast of events in the contemporary world, responding to them with Scripture as needed. Sinibaldo expounds:

> We are not to give equal value to God's word revealed and handed down through the generations and the daily word reported and experienced with the fresh voice of a journalist this morning. We don't just read the newspaper and figure out what to do about it on our own. Nor do we keep our head in the book and shut the doors to our churches and leave personal experience aside. We need a contemporary voice and one of wisdom that scripture provides.[25]

It is this balance that is lacking in views like those of Flowers, Vrbicek, and Wax. Awareness and application of Scripture concerning current events is not a threat to the gospel. Rather, it is the power of the gospel at work.

The Biblical Witness

Preaching on current events is not a fad of contemporary times but part of a long biblical tradition stretching back to creation. Since the garden of Eden, God has been invested in human history and activity. Since the earliest instances of humans speaking on behalf of God, it has been in response to the ongoing human situation. What are minimized as current events, headlines, or the news cycle often represent larger systemic forms of injustice. By addressing watershed moments that highlight these injustices or tackling the systems, we are doing the work of the kingdom of God. While modern evangelicalism often focuses on soteriology and the after-life, there is a long biblical tradition of speaking to the issues of this current world to bring us into alignment with the will of God. From the Egyptian enslavement of the children of Israel, to the mis-treatment of widows, orphans, and foreigners, to the exile in Babylon, to the first-century Roman occupation of Palestine, the biblical text gives witness to God caring about humanity's plight, sending prophets and preachers to address it. God has always been invested in current events and in politics! In the biblical text, those who spoke for God did not shy away from controversial topics. On the contrary, the full narrative of Scripture reads as a series of responses to the status quo with the revolutionary power of the prophetic voice.

When Moses said, "Let my people go" to the Egyptian pharaoh in Exodus 7, he was responding to the oppression of the Israelites. Their daily bondage and degradation filled the news cycle of ancient Egypt, and Moses was the vessel chosen by God to address it. Likewise, the ancient prophets from the eighth to the fifth cen-tury BCE each represented a godly response to the major current events of the time. Shifting religious views and practices, wars and foreign relations, the plight of exiles and refugees, the destruction of cities, and the rise and fall of political leaders were the current events. Had there been cable news in ancient Israel and Judah, these events would have had twenty-four-hour coverage with pundits opining on the various political ramifications. Had there been social media, these topics would each have been trending worldwide. In our time, cable news pundits give a political science perspective, and social media provides a popular culture perspective, but it is still the prophets of God who give a spiritual and theological perspective. The role of the prophets was to answer the pertinent question: What does God have to say about what is going on in our lives and in our nation? As crucial as Isaiah, Jeremiah, Amos, and Micah's voices were in their ancient context, the voice of today's preacher is crucial to responding to the newsworthy events that we face today.

In *The Hebrew Prophets and Their Social World*, Victor Matthews tracks the prophetic ministries in the Hebrew Bible from the early pre-monarchic period through the post-exilic period and the Hellenistic period in Daniel. The prophetic ministries of each era are marked by responses to the various political and cultural shifts within the society. Matthews notes, "On many occasions a prophet was forced to oppose the traditional views of the priestly community and the political agenda of the monarchy."[26] Not only did the prophets respond to current events, but they also specifically responded to politics and to culture, often in the uncomfortable position of being contrary to prevailing thought. The prophets voiced challenges to earthly authorities who ruled contrary to the will of God.

The voice of the prophet was a necessary check and balance to what was often the unquestioned voice of the ruling authorities. Matthews notes, "Within the political realm, the prophets often served as the conscience of the kings. It was their job to remind the monarch that he was not above the law and could be punished like any other Israelite for an infraction of the covenant (2 Samuel 12:1-15). Prophets also engaged in political acts."[27] Matthews provides several examples of the political activities of the prophets. "For instance, Elisha has one of his 'sons' anoint Jehu as king (2 Kings 9:1-13), and Jeremiah counsels King Zedekiah to accept Yahweh's judgment and surrender Jerusalem to the besieging Babylonians (Jeremiah 21:1-10; 38:17-18)."[28] Because we live in a polarized political climate, some preachers and pastors prefer to remain passive and neutral to avoid confrontations and disputes within their congregations. But in the biblical narrative, God has rarely remained neutral, particularly in the face of systemic injustice.

By providing sermonic responses to current events, preachers carry on the ancient tradition of speaking godly correction to ungodly leaders. Preachers also give correction to people who have been caught in the deceptive web of corruption and ungodliness, reminding them that neither governmental leaders nor popular culture are wholly representative of God. Whether speaking to a king, a pharaoh, Caesar, or the president of the United States, no one is bigger than God or beyond the reach of God's wrath when injustice continues. The task of the preacher, however, is more complex than correcting wrongs and proclaiming the coming wrath of God; we must tell the full gospel story that there is hope. We must remind the various purveyors of oppression that God is just, and that everywhere God's wrath can go, God's grace can go as well. We must tell hurting people that freedom is coming while empathizing with their current plight. God has repeatedly proven to be empathetic to the human condition by virtue of the incarnation. Preachers of the gospel must also incarnate this world to speak truth to power and empathy to the powerless. This is the heart of the kingdom of God, but to empathize, we must first recognize and respond to the current conditions that affect the contexts that we serve.

Twentieth-Century Preaching Examples

In *Prophetic Preaching: A Pastoral Approach*, Leonora Tubbs Tisdale details her extended research of the sermons preached by the first five pastors of the historic Riverside Church in New York. Riverside is an example of how a church and the preaching ministry of its pastors can effectively engage with current events to cause godly change in the world. Tisdale notes that "one of the striking things about the Riverside sermons is that you can literally read the history of our nation and world through them."[29] This is a remarkable testimony that other churches would do well to emulate. Riverside is a real-life illustration of what James Ward and Christine Ward mean in saying, "The preacher stands between the biblical text and the modern situation as a representative interpreter for the people of God."[30]

In addition to the historic sermons delivered by Riverside Church's pastors, guest preachers also delivered some important messages. Most notably among these is "Beyond Vietnam: A Time to Break Silence," delivered by Dr. Martin Luther King Jr. on April 4, 1967, exactly one year prior to his assassination. Indeed, King's delivery of that speech and his assassination one year later may be related to each other. The sanitizing of King in modern contexts may lead some to believe that he was always universally loved, but this was certainly not the case, especially late in his life when his fight for civil rights turned to a fight for economic justice for the poor and his opposition to the Vietnam War. Opposing the war in Vietnam amounted to taking on the federal government, a daunting task comparable to prophets of Israel approaching the ruling monarchs with rebuke. The Vietnam War was easily one of the top news stories of the late 1960s with polarizing views on each side. Even King himself played it safe for some time, not going public with his opposition, but early in the speech, he utters a quote that explains his change in tactic: "A time comes when silence is betrayal."[31] King clearly articulates why preachers of the gospel cannot shy away from the news cycle. The most controversial subjects are usually the most crucial, and silence accomplishes nothing.

King was aware of the magnitude and potential ramifications of his speech at Riverside. He made note that "even when pressed by the demands of inner truth, men do not easily assume the task of opposing their government's policy, especially in time of war. Nor does the human spirit move without great difficulty against all the apathy of conformist thought within one's own bosom and in the surrounding world."[32] He acknowledged the religious community's slowness in responding to an international crisis. "And we must rejoice as well, for surely this is the first time in our nation's history that a significant number of its religious leaders have chosen to move beyond the prophesying of smooth patriotism to the high grounds of a firm dissent based upon the mandates of conscience and the reading of history."[33]

The Riverside sermon was certainly not King's first foray into preaching about relevant current events; his ability to confront the issues of the time at just the right moment was the hallmark of his ministry. In the preface to his collection of sermons *Strength to Love*, King says:

> In these turbulent days of uncertainty the evils of war and of economic and racial injustice threaten the very survival of the human race. Indeed, we live in a day of grave crisis. The sermons in this volume have the present crisis as their background; and they have been selected for this volume because, in one way or another, they deal with the personal and collective problems that the crisis presents.[34]

This is the task in which every preacher should engage: to deal with the crises that our time presents. To be truly prophetic and relevant, the church must address not just current events but also the current social trends. The relevant events are often the product of long-brewing social issues that the church has neglected to address in a sufficient manner. For instance, it would not have been as crucial to craft a sermon addressing the police-involved homicides of Michael Brown, Tamir Rice, or Eric Garner and the resulting social unrest if the larger issue of police violence against people of color was already being addressed. It would not be as crucial to craft a sermon addressing a recent mass shooting if the larger issue of gun violence was already being addressed.

Current Event Engagement in Popular Media

Popular media have found success in what some branches of the church have been resistant to. Even comedies and fictitious dramas have found a way to stay relevant and connect with their audiences by engaging with current events and the news cycle. For instance, *Saturday Night Live* has solidified its position as a cultural institution. For nearly fifty years, the show has greeted American television audiences with the words "Live from New York, it's Saturday night." The show has had far more influence on American culture than one would expect a simple sketch comedy show to have. The show from its inception has had a finger on the pulse of the nation and has consistently responded to the various issues of the last forty-plus years at appropriate moments. Positioned to broadcast every Saturday night, the show for decades has served as a satirical recap of the events of the preceding week.

In the book *Saturday Night Live and American TV*, Ron Becker, Nick Marx, and Matt Sienkiewicz note that "from Chevy Chase's thin but arresting impersonation of President Gerald Ford in 1975 to Tina Fey's spot-on caricature of vice-presidential candidate Sarah Palin in 2008, Saturday Night Live has been the go-to location in US culture for humorous television commentary on presidents, presidential candidates, and election events."[35] The engagement in politics and current events has saved the show on many occasions, allowing its uniquely long run to continue. Becker, Marx, and Sienkiewicz reflect, "Campaign humor reasserts the program's cultural relevance, taking a show that has, over the years, periodically floundered with lackluster casts and poorly written sketches, and encouraging audiences (especially those outside its core youthful demographic) to care enough once again to watch, to share clips, and to use it for water cooler talk."[36] Because of a stance against preaching current events, many churches have missed opportunities to benefit from the type of cultural engagement that has sustained *Saturday Night Live*.

In the same way that *Saturday Night Live* has responded to current events with comedy and satire, the *Law and Order* franchises have found success by adapting fictional dramatic storylines based on real-life events. Like *Saturday Night Live*, *Law and Order* is a successful long-running franchise on the NBC network. The original *Law and Order* series ran for twenty years (1990–2010), and now the spinoff *Law and Order: SVU* itself has now crossed the twenty-year mark. The success of the franchise is largely due to the practice of presenting fictional narratives that are "ripped from the headlines." This strategy lends an air of familiarity to viewers who are already aware of similar real-life events that inspired the episodes.

Upon the original series' conclusion in 2010, the *New York Times* ran a feature highlighting some of the more popular episodes and their counterparts from the real-life news. The article confirms that "these are not just 'their stories.' Many of the 456 episodes that made up the stunning 20-year run of *Law and Order* were based on real, recognizable news stories—loosely based, at least."[37] Speaking of the show, creator Dick Wolf, and the staff of writers, the *Times* article says, "Mr. Wolf's writers combed through every daily paper, the tabloids always offering the best grist."[38] The writers simply responded to what was already on the minds and hearts of their audience.

The longevity and success of both *Saturday Night Live* and the *Law and Order* franchises are directly related to their ability to take the pulse of the nation and integrate current events that already weigh on people's consciousness. By engaging what is happening in the real world, the television shows fulfill their core purposes of humor, entertainment, suspense, and commentary while holding a large following from a cross-section of demographics. Our churches and preachers of the gospel can learn a lot from the strategy of these shows. To remain relevant for more than four decades in a rapidly changing culture and society is a feat that the church would do well to replicate.

When and How?

So, what are we to do with this information? If preaching on current events is an important part of a relevant gospel ministry, we are left with the question of *how*. While current-event preaching is permissible, useful, and in line with biblical and contemporary Christian witness, every current event sermon is not an effective one. Even when sermons are "ripped from the headlines," they must still be crafted through much prayer and careful examination of the biblical text. Preachers of the gospel are not mere journalists charged with finding and disseminating information—our task is to preach the gospel in a way that will address the current events that impact people's lives. Our task is to help our congregations view the rapidly changing culture through the timeless lens of God's Word. We have the awesome responsibility to speak on behalf of God through the relevant witness of Scripture. There is no current event that Scripture cannot speak to, but we must be careful to listen to what the Scriptures actually say. It is tempting to open with an anchoring scriptural text and then spend the remaining portion of the sermon opining or venting on the latest current event, but this temptation should be resisted. Ward and Ward give sound advice:

Our impulse is often simply to locate a text on the basis of a catchword association and develop a sermon more or less independently of the message of the text. In this way the text becomes a springboard, or perhaps a pretext, for our homiletical reflections rather than an integral part of them. When this happens, the application of the biblical text is unconvincing, and it detracts from the sermon rather than enhancing it, even though it seems to lend an aura of sanctity to it.[39]

The power of a sermon related to a current event is in the application of biblical truth, but preachers are not always successful in making that connection. To preach effectively in any context, the preacher must approach the text with a listening ear to find what God has to say and then work to reconcile that wisdom from the ancient text with the context of the present world.

Tisdale turns to Walter Brueggemann for insight. "For Brueggemann, prophetic witness is not primarily about addressing social or political issues, as important as it might be for preachers to do so. Rather, it is fundamentally about calling us as people of God to a radical reorientation of our worldview and consciousness so that we see and perceive the world as God sees it and have our hearts break over the things that break God's heart."[40] Every time there is tragedy, upheaval, unrest, political divisiveness, natural disasters, terrorism, racial injustice, or any other ground-shaking event in our society and culture, God invites us to see the world as God does. Seeing the world in its broken state through God's eyes should push us out of our comfort zones to pursue justice. Scripture shows us that God responds to injustice with action.

In the article "Current Events and When the Regular Sermon Just Won't Do," Rev. Scott Fuller reflects on his decision to rewrite his weekend sermon in the wake of the June 2015 tragic shooting at Mother Emmanuel AME Church. He remembers that his family was on vacation that week, and he had prepared everything in advance for the coming Sunday at the small church he served in rural Pennsylvania. He notes, "The bulletins were copied, the prayers composed, and the children's message outlined. I had even finished the sermon early. All I had to do was show up on Sunday morning."[41] Fuller knew a response of some type was required, but he wrestled with how to respond. He could have kept the service the same and simply mentioned the murders during announcements and in prayer. He could have reworked the sermon that he had already prepared to fit together with the tragedy, but ultimately, he chose the third option: to throw away the existing sermon and start over. He felt that the particularly horrific circumstances of the Mother Emmanuel shooting demanded something more.

From the shocking parallels of a murderer terrorizing a small church gathering to the racial motives that fueled the shooter, it was something that deeply affected the people of his congregation. Still, the decision to craft a sermon to specifically address a current event is the riskiest and should not be taken lightly. Fuller reflects on what he calls the "struggle between the twin poles of challenging my congregation and not rocking the boat."[42] While some situations require a response, some church members may take offense and make the job of the pastor more difficult. Fuller notes that "we all have colleagues and friends who have either landed in trouble with governing boards or in hot water with parishioners for taking stands on controversial issues."[43] Since at the time Fuller served as an interim pastor at what he described as a "small, aging, Caucasian church,"[44] discussions around racism in our country had the potential to be especially divisive and explosive, but he felt that this horror demanded the risk of potentially upsetting people.

Fuller poses four questions to ask before writing or rewriting a sermon to address a current event. First, "Does this situation affect the congregation, or the community in which the congregation resides?" Second, "Do the scriptures, the congregation's tradition, the revelation of the Holy Spirit, or the wisdom of the pastor and members of the congregation speak to this issue in a particularly powerful way?" Third, "Is this sermon going to help the congregation grow as the people of God?" Finally, "If the situation or issue is not addressed, will parishioners feel that I have missed an opportunity to connect the gospel with something that is weighing heavily on their hearts and minds? If little or nothing is said, will what *is* said ring hollow?"[45] These are valid questions that should constantly be on the heart of those with a weekly preaching assignment. However risky the subject matter that we address, we are ultimately accountable to God for what we say and do not say to the church.

The tragedies of this world can easily overwhelm our human emotions leading to anguish, so it is crucial when preaching on current events to not dive further into the depths of despair. A thin line exists between righteous anger that motivates action and crippling hopelessness that causes despair. Our human analogies of the events of the world can lead to fear, anxiety, and depression, but an effective presentation of the gospel will point to hope even in moments when lament is necessary.

The classic laments of the Psalms serve as good models on how to move from lament to action to praise. Psalm 13, for instance, in six verses runs through the full cycle of emotional expression. In the first two verses, the psalmist registers a complaint unto God by repeatedly asking the simple question, "How long?"

How long, Lord? Will you forget me forever?
How long will you hide your face from me?
How long must I wrestle with my thoughts
and day after day have sorrow in my heart?
How long will my enemy triumph over me? (Psalm 13:1-2, NIV)

In the middle verses, 3 and 4, the psalmist turns to petition:

Look on me and answer, LORD my God.
    Give light to my eyes, or I will sleep in death,
and my enemy will say, "I have overcome him,"
    and my foes will rejoice when I fall. (Psalm 13:3-4, NIV)

In this portion of the lament, the psalmist remains fearful, detailing the potential results of his predicament, but it has turned from a general "how long?" to specific ("answer me," "give light to my eyes"). Finally, in verses 5-6, the psalmist shifts dramatically from lament, fear, and despair to hope and praise:

But I trust in your unfailing love;
    my heart rejoices in your salvation.
I will sing the LORD's praise,
    for he has been good to me. (Psalm 13:5-6, NIV)

Like the psalmist, preachers cannot avoid bad news in the name of staying positive and upbeat. Preachers must rather confront the despair which presents itself through current events and the twenty-four-hour news cycle to move the collective spirit of the people from lament to analysis, to petition, and ultimately, to hope and praise.

I add that negative current events are not the only ones that the preacher should address and integrate into the sermons. Events in popular culture can cause great joy and can serve as metaphoric examples of the joy of the Lord. If a sporting event, popular movie, or TV show captivates the conscience of the people, one can fight the uphill battle of changing the subject, or one can choose to integrate them into a sermon on the weightier matters of the Spirit. This is what Jesus did by teaching through parables. This is what Paul did when he spoke of the "unknown God" to the Greeks in

Acts 17. Every event or cultural phenomenon provides an opportunity to point people to God. We cannot preach current events as singular events of themselves, but we must preach the gospel of Jesus Christ considering current events, and we view those current events through the lens of the gospel.

Reflection Questions before You Preach

1. Does this event qualify as a "major" social or cultural moment?

2. Paraphrasing the words of Martin Luther King Jr., would silence be betrayal in this moment?

3. Does this moment require a full sermon, or will a brief statement or prayer suffice?

4. What does God have to say about what is going on?

5. Am I interpreting the Bible through current events or current events through the Bible?

Notes

1. Charles Wesley, "A Charge to Keep I Have" (1762).

2. Andy Flowers, "Five Reasons Not to Preach About Current Events," *Transformed: Living the Gospel in an Everyday World* (blog), Western Seminary, originally published Sept. 27, 2017, https://web.archive.org/web/20211016140 642/https://transformedblog.westernseminary.edu/2017/09/27/5-reasons-not-preach-current-events/.

3. Ibid.

4. Ibid.

5. Benjamin Vrbicek, "When Should a Pastor Address a Current Event?", *For the Church* (blog), Midwestern Seminary, February 12, 2018, https://ftc.co/ resource-library/blog-entries/when-should-a-pastor-address-a-current event.

6. Ibid.

7. Ibid.

8. Ibid.

9. Ibid.

10. Ibid.

11. Ibid.

12. Ibid.

13. Trevin Wax, "When Should a Church Address a Current Event?", *The*

Gospel Coalition (blog), September 5, 2017, https://www.thegospelcoalition.org
/blogs/trevin-wax/when-should-a-church-address-a-current event/.

14. Ibid.
15. Ibid.
16. Ibid.
17. Ibid.
18. Ibid.
19. Ibid.
20. Ibid.
21. Ibid.
22. Ibid.
23. Geoff T. Sinibaldo, "On Barth, the Bible and the Newspaper," March 5, 2015, sinibaldo.wordpress.com, sinibaldo.wordpress.com/2015/03/05/on-barth-the-bible-and-the-newspaper/.
24. Original Karl Barth quote is from *Time*, May 1, 1966.
25. Sinibaldo.
26. Victor H. Matthews, *The Hebrew Prophets and Their Social World: An Introduction* (Grand Rapids, MI: Baker Academic, 2012), 31.
27. Ibid., 32.
28. Ibid.
29. Leonora Tubbs Tisdale, *Prophetic Preaching: A Pastoral Approach* (Louisville, KY: Westminster John Knox, 2010), 34–35.
30. James Ward and Christine Ward, *Preaching from the Prophets* (Nashville: Abingdon, 1995), 85.
31. Martin Luther King Jr., "Beyond Vietnam: A Time to Break Silence," Riverside Church, New York City, April 4, 1967, http://rcha.rutgers.edu/images/2016-2017/1960s/Documents/7.-RCHA-2016-The-Culture-of-the-Sixties-Martin-Luther-King-Jr.-Beyond-Vietnam-condensed.pdf.
32. Ibid.
33. Ibid.
34. Martin Luther King Jr., *Strength to Love* (Cleveland: Collins & World, 1963).
35. Ron Becker, Nick Marx, and Matt Sienkiewicz, eds., *Saturday Night Live and American TV* (Bloomington: Indiana University Press, 2013).
36. Ibid., 78.
37. Randee Dawn and Susan Green, "Ripped from the Headlines," *New York Times*, May 21, 2010, http://www.nytimes.com/slideshow/2010/05/21/nyregion/20100523-ripped-slideshow/s/20100523-ripped-slideshow-slide-4AX4.html.
38. Ibid.
39. Ward and Ward, 87.
40. Tisdale, 69, quoting Walter Brueggemann, *The Prophetic Imagination*

(Philadelphia: Fortress Press, 1978), 13.

41. Scott Fuller, "Sermon Tips: Current Events and When the Regular Sermon Just Won't Do," Pittsburgh Theological Seminary, August 20, 2015, https://www.pts.edu/blog/sermon-tips-current events/.

42. Ibid.

43. Ibid.

44. Ibid.

45. Ibid.

CHAPTER 2

The Normative Task of Hope

Preaching as Response to Racial Injustice

The purpose of addressing current events in sermons is not to update the congregation on the happenings of the world—social media and television do a fine job of that already. Events that necessitate sermonic responses are typically ones the congregation already knows about and has been deeply affected by. The preaching task is not to give information but to cause transformation through the life-changing message of the gospel. The transformative power to move beyond shock, grief, or trauma can be summed up in one word—*hope*. Without the redeeming presence of hope, sermons risk being susceptible to what Andy Flowers described as "politics fatigue."[1] Confusing a gospel sermon with common political punditry suggests an ineffective delivery of the message of hope, and without hope, a sermon is not a sermon at all.

Hope moves beyond the description of a problem or an explanation of why it exists. Hope lifts listeners out of the depths of despair and pushes them toward corrective action. The presence of hope has long been a defining characteristic of the Black preaching tradition. In this chapter, I show the centrality of hope as a guiding theology and the key goal of the preaching moment particularly when following incidents of racial trauma and unrest. Incidents of racial injustice can be especially traumatizing to Black congregations. In addition to the everyday, often subtle racism many endure, recent years have seen an uptick in public incidents of racial violence and a resurgence in public displays of white supremacy, aided by the proliferation of cell phone cameras and social media. Above all else, the effective delivery of hope is necessary for these moments. The purpose of delivering hope is not merely to comfort but to heal in preparation for the final, pragmatic task, which is action. The hope given during the sermon is what prepares the listener to act when the sermon is done.

The Four Tasks of Practical Theology

In *Practical Theology: An Introduction*, Richard R. Osmer presents four tasks of practical theology, which include the descriptive-empirical, the interpretive, the normative, and the pragmatic tasks. Put simply, the descriptive-empirical task answers the question "what is going on," the interpretive task answers "why is this going on," the normative task answers "what ought to be going on," and the pragmatic answers "how might we respond?" The preaching moment represents the crucial normative task and requires painting a picture of hope when addressing the turbulent events of contemporary society. Without hope, sermons responding to current events are merely extensions of the local or national news broadcast. The transformative power of hope is what makes preaching necessary and powerful.

Osmer makes no claim of originality in describing these four tasks, noting, "While the terms may differ, something like each of them is taught in clinical pastoral education, doctor of ministry courses, and courses on preaching, pastoral care, administration, Christian education and evangelism in schools of theology."[2] One of these parallel examples comes from Kenyatta Gilbert's "trivocal" approach (more on this in chapter 3).[3] The three parts of Gilbert's trivocal preaching are the priestly, the prophetic, and the sagely, while Osmer frames the descriptive-empirical task as "priestly listening," the interpretive task as "sagely wisdom," and the normative task as "prophetic discernment." While Gilbert focuses on the tasks specific to the preaching moment, Osmer extends the tasks to the wider disciplines of practical theology. Gilbert's trivocal approach does not have a fourth parallel description for the pragmatic task because this is the work of ministry that takes place once the sermon has concluded. When the trivocal tasks of preaching are completed, the congregants are equipped to carry out the fourth pragmatic task. The effective delivery of hope is the critical normative function of every sermon. It is possible and reasonable for a sermon to address each of the four tasks including communicating action steps for a pragmatic response. Without painting the picture of a hopeful future rooted in the current context, the sermon has failed at its primary normative task. Sermons can embody many functions and styles; some are didactic, others are more metaphoric, some are thematic, and others are expository. Whatever style is used to communicate the gospel, the gospel by its very essence and definition must include a normative vision of hope.

While challenging the privileged and confronting oppression in all forms are also crucial, the net result of every sermon should be hope for a more righteous future and motivation for the work that will bring it to pass. The effective delivery of hope is especially important when addressing marginalized populations. Everyone needs hope, but it is exponentially more important to those who are actively suffering. This truth can be applied to various populations: women, immigrants, LGBTQ+, the poor, victims of racial injustice, and many others. While many formats address these societal issues in various forms like articles, speeches, books, policy, and legislative documents, the normative hope that comes from the preaching of the gospel cannot be minimized. Osmer's framework shows the delivery of hope as preaching's crucial normative task with an emphasis on the context of being Black in America. Using non-sermonic examples of the descriptive-empirical and interpretive tasks, we examine how hope as the normative task is necessary for sermons that respond to current events.

Describing without Uplifting
(the Descriptive-Empirical Task)

In the memoir *Between the World and Me*, Ta-Nehisi Coates addresses the experience of being Black in America. Much like James Baldwin in *The Fire Next Time*,[4] Coates pens a first-person letter to a young Black man (his son, in Coates's case) as an existential opus reflecting on his experience of the current times. By using the open letter format, Coates gives us a window into his emotions. The imagery is tangible and the pain palpable as he writes to his son. *Between the World and Me* represents what Osmer describes as the descriptive-empirical task. While Coates gives an in-depth description of his life as a Black man in America, he does not move much past description. The text provides no real examination of the root causes of his struggle or paints a picture of what the ideal looks like and offers no practical steps to achieve it. While the book is uniquely creative in its presentation and powerful in expressing Coates's raw and charged emotions, the key element of hope, crucial in a sermon, is missing. While not a sermon, Coates's book is a cautionary tale of the hopelessness that tempts those who actively address the various ills of society.

The open letter can be an effective way to communicate prophetic truth. In *Prophetic Preaching: A Pastoral Approach*, Leonora Tubbs Tisdale highlights two examples of effective use of the open letter format.[5] In "Paul's Letter to American Christians," Martin Luther King Jr. pens a first-person letter in the voice of Paul of Tarsus directed at American Christians in the mid-twentieth century. The familiar style of the Pauline epistle was used to sermonically address issues pertinent to King's contemporary context. Tisdale also highlighted "An Open Letter to Billy Graham" by Earnest Campbell, former pastor of the Riverside Church in Manhattan. In that sermon/letter, Campbell openly challenged Billy Graham to use his influence to speak out against the war in Vietnam. Unlike

Between the World and Me, both sermonic examples have a call to action and a normative claim of hope.

The Willful Rejection of Hope

Coates does not casually omit hope as an oversight or an incomplete thought; he willfully and vocally challenges the notion that we should have hope at all. At the close of an interview by a popular news program amid the Ferguson protests, the host flashed a widely shared picture of a tearful Black boy hugging a white police officer. He then asked Coates about hope, and Coates saw this as a mark of failure on his part. He viewed hope as a distraction from the current plight or as missing the point rather than as a catalyst to spur toward the arduous task of change. This is not merely a part of Coates's disposition but a generational practice in his family line. Reflecting on the news that there would be no charges in the police killing of Eric Gardner, Coates says to his son, "I heard you crying. I came in five minutes after, and I didn't hug you, and I didn't comfort you, because I thought it would be wrong to comfort you. I did not tell you that it would be okay, because I have never believed it would be okay."[6]

Coates attributes this practice to his own parents, stating, "This rejection was a gift from your grandparents, who never tried to console me with ideas of an afterlife."[7] Therein lies the heart of the issue. Coates illustrates that the lack of hope is a direct byproduct of an ill-conceived view of God. Hope and faith are intrinsically connected to each other, and an atheistic worldview naturally lends itself to hopelessness. In the words of Edward Mote's famous 1834 hymn, "My hope is built on nothing less than Jesus' blood and righteousness. I dare not trust the sweetest frame, but wholly lean on Jesus's name. On Christ the solid Rock I stand; all other ground is sinking sand."[8] Coates's willful rejection of hope is a living example of Mote's metaphoric "sinking sand." His rejection of hope cannot be separated from his rejection of God.

The Lost Art of Lament

Coates is, however, not above questioning his own hopelessness. Upon meeting Mable Jones, the mother of Prince Jones, his college friend whose life was taken by the police, Coates wrestled with the notion that by rejecting hope he was missing out on something. He states, "I often wonder if in that distance I've missed something, some notions of cosmic hope, some wisdom beyond my mean physical perception of the world, something beyond the body, that I might have transmitted to you. I wondered this, at that particular moment, because something beyond anything I have ever understood drove Mable Jones to an exceptional life."[9] He frames this encounter with Jones in the final chapter (the shortest of the three), positioning it as the volta, a term in poetry used to describe a rhetorical shift or sudden turn in emotion. This same turn is common among the Psalms of lament, like the "But I have trusted in thy mercy" of Psalm 13:5 after the "how long?" of verses 1 through 4 (see chapter 1).

Between the World and Me is at its core a contemporary lament. The lament is a lost art in many contemporary churches, long abandoned in favor of the gospel of positivity. In many ways, this overemphasis on positivity (i.e., "always seeing the bright side of life") could be exactly what Coates and those like him have rebelled against. There is a strong line of delineation between hope amid suffering and what Karl Marx would describe as "an opium of the people."[10] Rather than work through the suffering of this world anchored in the "already" and "not yet" hope of Jesus Christ, some choose to bury their heads in the sand of positivity while the world around them burns. Contrary to this ideology, lament is a necessary step on the road to hope. Through the process of open lament, Coates found his way to several small glimmers of hope, from self-education, to writing, to finding love on Howard's campus, to Mable Jones. But each of those glimmers proved fleeting and ultimately gave way to a pessimistic outlook. Hope not based on the eternality of God consistently proves to be temporary. Lament is a powerful tool, but it must give way to hope. Hopelessness is a pervasive force, consuming when left unresolved.

Explaining without Transforming (the Interpretive Task)

If Coates is stuck on the descriptive-empirical task, then Michelle Alexander lands on the interpretive task. *The New Jim Crow: Mass Incarceration in the Age of Colorblindness* is a masterpiece of interpretive work. While Coates describes his life as a Black man, Alexander delves into the root causes that contribute to the marginalization of Blacks in America. She offers statistics, historic narratives, and real-world testimonies that move the conversation from what to why. From slavery to Jim Crow to the current mass incarceration, Alexander paints the picture of the changing political and social climate that has produced the successive forms of oppression that still deeply affect American society.

In the book, Alexander provides an analogy of America's need for a deeper understanding of racial dynamics. She compares the study of racism with the wires of a bird cage. Examining one wire will not show how and why the bird is trapped. The large number of intersecting wires keeps the bird confined. In this analogy, Coates's descriptive-empirical function is one wire of the cage—the "wire" of experience as a Black man in the twentieth and twenty-first centuries. By examining the social, political, and historic landscape that has produced the contemporary Black experience, Alexander has effectively constructed the "large number of wires" that cage the proverbial bird. This is the interpretive task of which Osmer speaks. Coates effectively communicates the what while Alexander does the work of finding the why. However, what and why are both insufficient in the task of responding to racial injustices—a normative claim is necessary for moving the needle forward.

It is tempting to move directly from the descriptive-empirical and interpretive tasks to the pragmatic task. Knowing what the issue is and knowing the root causes of the issue naturally produce a desire to address the root causes to effect change, but the pragmatic task depends on first knowing what the end goal is. Knowing what the ideal looks like is crucial for developing a pragmatic strategy. To create policy based on description and interpretation is to throw darts in the dark. Sadly, this is largely what happened in the post–civil rights years in America. What began as a moral movement led by preachers in churches became a policy movement led by lawyers and politicians.

Alexander addresses this in *The New Jim Crow* by showing the transition from grassroots organizing largely in churches and other faith-based community organizations to policy discussion behind the closed doors of courtrooms. She notes, "Instead of a moral crusade, the movement became an almost purely legal crusade."[11] Instead of preachers and community activists, lawyers became viewed as "the most important players in racial justice advocacy."[12] This perception became even more prominent after the Civil Rights Act of 1965. Not only did the focus move from the streets to the courtroom, but the pulpit was circumvented altogether.

The preached word, therefore, remains the crucial normative task of giving hope for a brighter future to those who are suffering. The pragmatic act of policy development detached from the morally normative task of preaching separates the end result from the very ones who would benefit from the change. From a spiritual standpoint, pragmatic policy development is insufficient when it has no guidance from the God of the oppressed, who fights alongside us for our liberty. Make no mistake—this is a spiritual fight, and our hope comes from this.

As preachers of the gospel, our responsibility is to consider the descriptive-empirical account given by Coates and the interpretive account given by Alexander, and then present hope as a normative response guided by the Holy Spirit and Scripture. Osmer cites practical theologian Thomas Long's emphasis on priestly listening. In *The Witness of Preaching*, Long notes that "when preachers turn to the Bible to prepare their sermons, they must bring with them an awareness of the life situations of the hearers, for preaching 'speaks to particular people in the concrete circumstances of their lives.'"[13] The firsthand testimonial of Coates and the interpretive research of Alexander (and others like them) should inform preachers when addressing contemporary social issues. By first listening to their voices, we can effectively respond with the message of hope.

Showing What Should Be
(Hope as the Normative Task)

When life on the social and racial margins is challenging and the daily news cycle is filled with chaos, confusion, and uncertainty, the normative task casts a vision for peace and a restorative future. The normative task is, in short, the effective delivery of hope. Whether responding to racial injustice, a tragedy, or governmental or economic unrest, the listening congregation needs more than a current news report or a pseudo-theological explanation of why the world is the way it is. They need a clear picture of what the world can and should look like. Hope fills this normative task, and without it, a sermon responding to current events (or any other sermon for that matter) is incomplete. To understand the urgency of hope in contemporary sermons, we must examine the origins of hope in African American preaching.

In *The Motif of Hope in African American Preaching during Slavery and the Post–Civil War Era*, Wayne E. Croft Sr. explores the use of hope as a motif in African American preaching during slavery (1803–1865) and the post–Civil War period (1865–1896). While the centrality of hope in African American preaching is often asserted, Croft rigorously investigates this claim by examining early examples of African American preaching from the nineteenth century. In doing so, Croft illustrates how the delivery of hope is especially crucial for preaching in the African American tradition. Since the beginning, Black preaching in America has responded to the daily cycle of oppression and struggle with the gospel's life-giving power of hope.

The History of Hope

Hope is always an appropriate response to current events because hope is the realization of the defiant Black Christian spirit of "in spite of." Whatever is happening locally, nationally, or internationally, whatever is being reported in the headlines, whatever the struggles of daily life, hope exists in spite of current conditions. Henry H. Mitchell states that "the genius of Black preaching has been its capacity to generate celebration despite circumstances."[14]

In *Come Sunday: The Liturgy of Zion*, William B. McClain says, "No matter how dark a picture has been painted or how gloomy, there is always a 'but' or a 'nevertheless' or an element in the climax of the sermon that suggests holding on, marching forward, going through, or overcoming."[15] Black preaching has always lived in the "nevertheless" along with the hopeful proclamation of all marginalized people. Otis Moss III calls this "Blues Sensibilities." Blue note preaching, according to Moss, is "prophetic preaching—preaching about tragedy, but refusing to fall into despair."[16] Croft points to the great spiritual of the Black church:

> There's a bright side somewhere,
> There's a bright side somewhere,
> Don't you rest until you find it,
> There's a bright side somewhere.

Giving hope is the singular task of preaching the gospel. The role of hope in preaching is to paint the picture of that "somewhere" before it is found. The hope of the resurrection despite the agony of the cross is the central claim of the gospel and applicable to the many crosses that we bear in our own lives.

Hope for This Life and the Life to Come

While hope is central to Black preaching, different types of hope can be offered. The contrasts and intersections of hope for this life and hope for the life to come are key to consider. What Croft describes as "other-worldly" sermons were preached to encourage the enslaved to "endure present problems and pain, not to resist slavery but to look forward to a better life in the afterworld."[17] Key figures such as George Liele, Denmark Vesey, and Nat Turner rose up in protest of an exclusively other-worldly view of hope. However, Croft points to the nuance between the two views being present in that era. For instance, Frederick Douglass stated that for him and many fellow enslaved people, the song "O Canaan, sweet Canaan/I am bound for the land of Canaan" symbolized "something more than a hope of reaching heaven. We meant to reach the North, and the North was our Canaan."[18] In this case, this-worldly hope was expressed using other-worldly metaphors.

In *Black Theology and Black Power*, James H. Cone rejects the appeal to the next life as a "lack of hope" and views Black theology as a theology of hope for this life.[19] He argues that post–Civil War Black preachers taught Blacks to forget this-worldly hope and look to other-worldly hope for freedom and equality.[20] Croft, however, pushes back on this argument, showing that in the sermons of Daniel Payne and John Jasper, both dimensions of hope are present. Though from the nineteenth century, these preachers exemplify contrasting approaches to the normative task of hope when responding to current events. The delivery of hope should always consider the context of the situation being responded to. Jasper at a funeral called for one approach, Payne upon the emancipation of slaves in DC called for another, but in every situation, the preacher must answer the question, how can I give hope through the gospel?

Beyond Preaching (the Pragmatic Task)

The collective works of Howard Thurman speak to the necessity of hope for the proverbial man with his "back against the wall." Thurman shows the condition of the downtrodden to be a matter of utmost spiritual importance, and the need for preachers to address these conditions. The story of Jesus has much to say to the disinherited, but Thurman highlighted the relative silence of the religion of Jesus on these matters. In *Jesus and the Disinherited* Thurman notes, "The masses of the people are poor. If we dare take the position that in Jesus there was at work some radical destiny, it would be safe to say that in his poverty he was more truly Son of man than he could have been if the incident of family or birth had made him a rich son of Israel."[21] The incarnation was God showing love to humanity by becoming a poor man. The core of the gospel has always been good news to the poor—this message has been embedded in Christianity since the beginning, but that message is often distorted and silenced. The task of the twenty-first-century preacher is to recover the voice of hope as a response to ongoing hopelessness. Thurman's life and writings emphasized the task of hope through two guiding principles: recognizing the image of God in all people, and the will to overcome hatred with love.

The notion of God siding with the oppressed did not originate with Cone's classic 1975 book—it was alive and central in the writings of Thurman generations before. Thurman does not just speak of God being on the side of the oppressed; he emphasizes the godliness inherent in their own beings. The *imago Dei* is a defining characteristic of Thurman's prophetic writings, and the belief that all are made in the image of God is the foundational premise that guides the totality of Thurman's work. The work of the preacher is to stabilize the ego of the disinherited by identifying their connection to God. Thurman says:

> If a man's ego has been stabilized, resulting in a sure grounding of his sense of personal worth and dignity, then he is in a position to appraise his own intrinsic powers, gifts, talents, and abilities. He no longer views his equipment through the darkened lenses of those who are largely responsible for his social predicament. He can think of himself with some measure of detachment from the shackles of his immediate world.[22]

The image of God in the underclass is most evident in the life of Jesus himself. Thurman notes that Jesus himself was a poor Jew in first-century Roman-occupied Palestine, which means he was "a member of a minority group in the midst of a larger dominant and controlling group."[23] Surely the Son of God could have incarnated in the social status of his choosing, but God chose a poor Jewish carpenter in Roman-ruled Palestine. This condition of Jesus's birth is significant, as it shores up the premise that all, including the poor and disenfranchised, are in the image of God. Surely if the Son of God in the flesh was a poor minority, the rest of society's marginalized could see the image of God in themselves. Jesus's poverty and low social status were not peripheral to his existence; they were necessary for his greater purpose.

However, the *imago Dei* is not present just in the disinherited but in all of humanity, including those who are the perpetuators of oppression. This is where Thurman's work truly challenges. To see the image of God in oneself is not enough; we must also work to overcome hatred with love to see God even in one's enemies. As a child of the Jim Crow South, Thurman could have given in to his base desires for anger, hatred, and retaliation. Remarkably, he goes deeper, challenging the listener toward the harder work of progress and reconciliation. In doing so, he calls the preacher and church at large to the pragmatic task and offers a deeper hope fueled by action. Even in the absence of larger social movements, the task of preaching should offer hope to the poor and forgotten. But the response of the church and the preacher must go beyond just preaching. Thurman says, "Mere preaching is not enough. What are words, however sacred and powerful, in the presence of the grim facts of the daily struggle to survive? Any attempt to deal with this situation on a basis of values that disregard the struggle for survival appears to be in itself a compromise with life."[24] Preaching's normative task of hope is crucial whether responding to singular events, larger social movements, or the daily context of life on the margins, but the aim should always be to motivate action.

Reflection Questions before You Preach

1. Does this message give information or inspire transformation?
2. Does this message achieve the central task of giving hope to the listener?
3. Have I rushed to hope at the expense of thoughtful lament?
4. Is there a balance of hope for the present and hope for the life to come?
5. Has enough hope been given for the listener to carry out the next step of pragmatic action?

Notes

1. Andy Flowers, "Five Reasons Not to Preach About Current Events," *Transformed: Living the Gospel in an Everyday World* (blog), Western Seminary, originally published 9/27/2017, https://web.archive.org/web/20211016140642/ https://transformedblog.westernseminary.edu/2017/09/27/5-reasons-not-preach-current-events/

2. Richard R. Osmer, *Practical Theology: An Introduction* (Grand Rapids, MI: Eerdmans, 2008), Kindle, 95–98.

3. Kenyatta Gilbert, *The Journey and Promise of African American Preaching* (Minneapolis: Fortress Press, 2011).

4. James Baldwin, *The Fire Next Time* (New York: The Dial Press, 1963).

5. Lenora Tubbs Tisdale, *Prophetic Preaching: A Pastoral Approach* (Louisville, KY: Westminster John Knox, 2010).

6. Ta-Nehisi Coates, *Between the World and Me* (New York: Spiegel & Grau, 2015), 11.

7. Ibid.

8. Edward Mote, "The Solid Rock" (1834).

9. Coates, 139.

10. Karl Marx, *Critique of Hegel's Philosophy of Right* (1843).

11. Michelle Alexander, *The New Jim Crow: Mass Incarceration in the Age of Colorblindness* (New York: The New Press, 2012), 225.

12. Ibid.

13. Osmer, 469, quoting Thomas G. Long, *The Witness of Preaching* (Louisville, KY: Westminster John Knox, 2003), 55.

14. Henry H. Mitchell, *Celebration and Experience in Preaching* (Nashville: Abingdon, 1990), 12.

15. William B. McClain, *Come Sunday: The Liturgy of Zion* (Nashville: Abingdon, 1990), 69–70.

16. Otis Moss III, *Blue Note Preaching in a Post-Soul World: Finding Hope in an Age of Despair* (Louisville, KY: Westminster John Knox, 2015).

17. Wayne E. Croft Sr., *The Motif of Hope in African American Preaching during Slavery and the Post–Civil War Era* (Lanham, MD: Lexington Books, 2017), 47.

18. Frederick Douglass, *Life and Times of Frederick Douglass* (rev. ed., 1892; reprint ed., New York: Collier, 1962), 159.

19. James H. Cone, *Black Theology and Black Power* (New York: Seabury Press, 1969; reprint ed., Maryknoll, NY: Orbis Books, 2005).

20. Ibid., 105.

21. Howard Thurman, *Jesus and the Disinherited* (New York: Abingdon, 1949), 17.

22. Ibid., 53.

23. Ibid., 18.

24. Howard Thurman, *With Head and Heart: The Autobiography of Howard Thurman* (New York: Harcourt Brace, 1979), 69.

CHAPTER 3

Crafting Controversial Content

Risk and Redemption in
Preaching Current Events

While hope is essential when addressing current events, the preaching moment requires more than a rush to hope. A willingness to take risks is essential when addressing current events or cultural movements. The nature of the news cycle implies that the events and issues that arise are new, groundbreaking, and often shocking. Whether from a political bombshell or a local or national tragedy, emotions and polarized views arise from the point of the breaking news. Journalistic integrity requires neutrality. Conversely, preaching with power often requires choosing a position or side. Risk is always involved in choosing sides, whether personal and vocational risks to the preacher or institutional risks to the congregation. To avoid potentially catastrophic fallout, preaching on controversial subjects requires wisdom and nuance.

Marvin McMickle says, "Sometimes a sermon must be preached that embraces matters that are controversial and unpopular with the listeners. Such a sermon is not always planned . . . Often such a sermon is required in response to events that have unexpectedly occurred whether in the surrounding community or somewhere in the country or world."[1] However, while the need to speak truth to power is constant, McMickle also warns, "Do not try to confront Pharaoh every Sunday."[2] Addressing current events in a polarized political and social climate is a risky endeavor, but the gospel mandates that risk be taken in pursuit of communal redemption. Balance in presentation is required to faithfully address current events and related controversies in the preaching of the gospel. A balanced approach when responding to significant moments and movements is a rich and storied part of the Black preaching tradition from which others can learn.

Getting Started: The Call to Awareness and Action

In *The Making of a Preacher: Five Essentials for Ministers Today*, Marvin A. McMickle offers a five-step process for the formation of preachers: hearing the call, confessing your character, claiming your content, knowing your context, and facing the consequences. The call is the tangible leading by the voice of God that causes preachers to enter the vocation. Character deals with the quality of the preacher as a person both before and after the call to ministry. Claiming your content involves the themes and topics included in a preacher's schedule of sermons, while knowing your context involves the geographic or cultural location in which preaching occurs. Finally, facing the consequences confronts the reality that preaching relevant contextual sermons bears a risk. Addressing current issues with relevant sermonic content means some will likely reject the message. McMickle suggests that part of being made into a preacher involves dealing with the sometimes predictable, sometimes unexpected consequences of preaching. Effective preaching does not always mean popular preaching—part of the making of a preacher is coming to terms with this reality.

Awareness of the Present Moment

McMickle is clear that effective preaching must be done with what Paul Tillich calls "an awareness of the current moment."[3] He expounds, "Preaching does not occur in a sociopolitical void where the circumstances that surround both the pulpit and the pew are irrelevant. Quite to the contrary, there must always be a clear understanding of the ways in which the context of our sermons has immediacy and relevance to the contexts in which people live every day."[4] This "present moment" constitutes the context of preaching, and preaching is always done in context. A sermon that does not address context is irrelevant. An irrelevant sermon may be entertaining or performative, but it lacks the power to truly cause the change needed as a response to the gospel message. Awareness of the present moment is not a tool to fuel gimmickry or capture the fleeting attention of churchgoers; it is the substance of the gospel itself and the power thereof. Sadly, irrelevant sermons are more the norm than the exception. Theologian Paul Lehmann says, "Most sermons are notably irrelevant. Sermons—even carefully crafted ones—are nearly always eventless. They are a compound of either the obvious and the trivial, or the learned and the commonplace—or both—on the move from the latitudinous to the platitudinous. Everybody likes to hear what everybody knows— and effectively dismissed as not worth bothering about."[5] McMickle suggests sermons that address the current context may be controversial but are seldom if ever irrelevant.

Preaching in context requires identifying and naming the context in which we find ourselves. McMickle says, "The context in which preaching is occurring in the twenty-first century is far more influenced by CNN and ESPN, by Netflix and Hulu, by podcasts and other forms of social media than it is by what is being preached from the pulpits of churches across the United States."[6] To be effective in twenty-first-century preaching means understanding this reality and interact with the messages that the listeners are already hearing, showing why the gospel matters. The essential purpose of current event preaching is to bring prophetic critique to the events that are already at the forefront of the listeners' minds.

Keeping up with passing trends is insufficient for the task. Relevant preaching is not defined by popular culture but by responding to more substantial shifts in society with the steadying messages of love, justice, and freedom through Christ. McMickle says, "Preachers are not fully made until they have incorporated into their preaching God's demand for the liberation of oppressed people across this country and around the world."[7] Effective communication of God's demand for the liberation of oppressed people requires a sense of where oppression is currently occurring and the will to confront it. While the Black church is a known voice fighting the racism inflicted on our own community, the work of preachers should not be confined to the oppression that affects them or their own community. A calling to preach means a burning desire to correct oppression wherever it occurs by proclaiming the message of liberty for all captives through Jesus Christ.

Beyond the Moment: Responding to Social Movements

Single events often birth larger social movements. *Be My Witness*, McMickle's earlier book, suggests that preachers should engage in bold speech based on the Greek word *parrhesia*. Cornel West defines *parrhesia* as "speaking the truth boldly and freely without any regard for the speaker's safety and security."[8] This is precisely what preachers should aim to do in the face of the numerous issues facing this generation. McMickle suggests that a good way to think about *parrhesia* in the twenty-first century is to consider a line spoken by President Barack Obama in his second inaugural address. While referring to three major movements for freedom and equality, Obama said the struggle extended "from Seneca Falls, to Selma, to Stonewall."[9] Seneca Falls refers to the Women's Convention held in Seneca Falls, New York, in 1848, which birthed the larger movement for women's rights. Selma, the historic 1965 march from Selma to Montgomery, Alabama, is emblematic of the larger civil rights movement for Black Americans. Stonewall refers to the police raid and resistance in 1969 at the Stonewall nightclub in New York City, which was a catalyst in the movement for LGBTQ+ rights. In addition to the three events invoked by President Obama, McMickle adds the more recent Standing Rock as symbolic of larger environmental concerns. Standing Rock refers to the protest by the Lakota and thousands of allies who opposed the construction of an oil pipeline through the Standing Rock Indian Reservation near Bismarck, North Dakota, as well as the larger struggle for human rights and environmental protections.

Continuing the alliterative litany of movements, I add Sanford to the list. Sanford, Florida, is the location where Trayvon Martin was killed by George Zimmerman, and the BLM movement was birthed. Seneca Falls, Selma, Stonewall, Standing Rock, Sanford . . . each of these geographic locations is emblematic of larger movements for justice in need of a bold response by preachers of the gospel. McMickle challenges preachers to consider these opportunities for bold speech and any others that may arise. He cautions, "This is not a call to address these topics every Sunday . . . while a good pastor will address a wide range of other topics, a faithful pastor must address issues such as these on a regular basis."[10]

Trivocal Versatility

In *The Journey and Promise of African American Preaching*, Kenyatta Gilbert agrees with McMickle that pastors should not try to "confront Pharaoh every Sunday."[11] While prophetic preaching that speaks truth to power and confronts societal ills is necessary, it must be balanced with other approaches. In addition to the prophetic voice, Gilbert points to the priestly voice and the sagely voice, which together make up what he calls trivocal preaching.

The prophetic voice, when used effectively, fulfills the normative task of hope. Gilbert describes the prophetic word as "a word of relentless hope."[12] More than offering a benign vision of hope, the prophetic voice calls the people to participate in a hopeful future anchored in the just will of God. The voice of the prophet is one of correction, and the task is transforming injustice into justice. Gilbert says, "The common thread of all prophetic preaching is the recognition of injustice, and that the preacher will name injustice for what it is, and what justice should be."[13] Prophetic preaching, by its nature, is current event preaching because it is a wholly contextual enterprise that takes inventory of the current culture and aligns it with God's will. Whether speaking to kings, presidents, or wayward common folk, the prophet's task is to confront the sin of injustice and challenge the offenders to repent. Prophets are rarely popular, which is why those in pastoral ministry cannot preach prophetic sermons every Sunday. The need to challenge and confront must be balanced with the need to nurture and comfort.

While prophetic preaching automatically lends itself to current event response, the priestly voice is equally important, particularly when responding to local or national tragedies. A natural disaster, terrorist attack, or death of a public figure may not be the time for a prophetic rebuke. When the congregation is in mourning, the prophetic voice's sharp critique is not what is necessary but rather the calming priestly voice inviting the congregation to prayer and communal strength. Gilbert identifies calling the gathered community to prayer as the most important function of the priestly voice. The prophetic voice is the voice of challenge, while the priestly voice is one of healing and renewed consecration. No pastor can be effective while functioning as a full-time prophet. The role of pastoring requires more than crying out in the wilderness or speaking truth to power—it requires loving support. The priestly voice draws the listeners into encounters with God whereby they can access healing, peace, and divine restoration. Still, Gilbert notes, "Many would claim that the priestly voice is primarily the voice of religious and communal socialization, which focuses almost entirely on parishioner needs while having little impact on the wider society."[14] However, to change the world, disciples must first experience the life-changing power of

God in their own lives, and the priestly voice invites listeners into this process.

The sagely voice is the strangest one to reconcile with contemporary culture and the daily news cycle because it is concerned with the past, not the present or future. Gilbert describes the sagely voice as the most overlooked of the three voices due to "Black religious practices that are preoccupied with the ethos of contemporary culture, which ascribes greater worth to present-future preaching interests."[15] The priestly voice ministers to present needs and the prophetic voice points to a more just future, while the sagely voice "interprets the congregation's historical and cultural legacy, namely, its archival materials, and seeks to decode the complex signs, symbols, and texts of a congregation's worship life."[16] The sagely voice preserves the worship, traditions, and values of local congregations and faith traditions. The sagely voice is every bit as crucial in responding to current events as the priestly and prophetic voices. Both the present and the future have been set in motion by the legacy of the past. Context is not defined by the current position but by reconciling our current position with what has already happened and what is still to come. If the prophetic voice represents "prophetic discernment," the sagely voice represents the crucial act of prophetic remembrance. Prophetic discernment points toward a hopeful future. Prophetic remembrance recalls that we have been through this before and the same God who brought us out then is faithful to do it again.

Addressing Domains of Experience

While Gilbert frames the Black preaching voice as trivocal, in *The Heart of Black Preaching*, Cleophas LaRue explores the contrasting voices of the Black pulpit in more detail through what he terms domains of experience. He defines a domain as "a sphere or realm that covers a broad but specified area of Black experience and also provides a category for sermonic reflection, creation, and organization."[17] In LaRue's model, the addressing of experience is the driving force behind Black preaching, within which he identifies five specific domains: personal piety, care of the soul, social justice, corporate concerns, and maintenance of the institutional church.

Personal piety emphasizes "heart religion, the centrality of the Bible for faith and life, the royal priesthood of the laity, and strict morality."[18] LaRue describes this as the most common of the domains, and he points to the evangelical revivalism of the late eighteenth and early nineteenth centuries as the point of origin for Black attraction to personal piety. Indeed, this domain is often synonymous with Christian discipleship in the Black church. LaRue says, "Many Blacks are convinced that they have not heard the gospel if it does not address some aspect of life as it is lived in this domain. Even ministers who are known for their active participation on the social justice front preach sermons from time to time that have as their central focus some matter related to personal piety."[19]

Care of the soul means addressing the area of experience focused on personal well-being. LaRue clarifies that it is, however, "more than mere comfort for the bereaved, forgiveness for the guilty, and help for the sick and needy; it is preeminently the renewal of life in the image of Christ."[20] Beyond giving comfort, this domain works to redirect life in response to lived experiences.

Experiences pertaining to racism, sexism, ageism, and other forms of discrimination fall within the scope of social justice. LaRue points to racial justice as the most prominent component of the social justice domain in the Black church experience noting, "Those who preach out of this domain view God as the source of social justice and are absolutely certain that God's Power is on their side in their quest for social reform."[21]

The concept of corporate concerns recognizes that "certain issues and interests in Black life arise out of its unique history and cultural experiences in this country."[22] This domain often centers on

exhortations of self-help, uplift, and racial solidarity. LaRue speci-
fies, "Unlike the domain of social justice, which seeks the common
good of all, the corporate concerns domain is specifically geared to
Black interests."[23] This domain is based on the notion that some
issues in the Black community are best addressed in the company
of other Blacks who have shared in the experience. While the
domain of community concerns can often overlap with the
prophetic voice of social justice, by calling upon the history, culture,
and joined experience of the Black American community this
domain exemplifies what Gilbert calls the sagely voice.

Likewise, maintenance of the institutional church fits the description of Gilbert's sagely voice. This domain is charged with the care
of the Black church as the center of Black culture. LaRue notes,
"Owing to the historical importance of the Black church in the
African American community, Blacks, by and large, experience
church not simply as a place to attend worship but as a way of
life."[24] The institutional church is maintained by recalling its history and significance in the lives of the listening congregation. LaRue
says, "Since many of the vital, life altering experiences of parishioners occur within the context of the Institutional church, much
preaching in Black pulpits is directed toward the maintenance of
the institution."[25] The maintenance of the institutional church is
framed as imperative for the continuance of ministry toward a
hopeful future. This domain reminds us of how the church has historically worked toward hope and reminds us of the necessity to
support the continuation of that work.

LaRue's aim in detailing the domains of experience is to show the
distinctive of Black preaching, even considering its variety of
scope. The distinctiveness of Black preaching comes from the intersection of experience and scriptural interpretation. By necessity, the
Black hermeneutics has always been one response to current
events. LaRue says, "The distinctive power of Black preaching is
tied directly to what Blacks believe about God's proactive interven-

tion and involvement in their experiences."[26] This distinctive power works to link what Scripture reveals about God to the daily circumstances of life, particularly life on the margins of society.

Confronting Political Power

The distinctive of biblical prophets was their willingness to confront corrupt and ungodly rulers of nations. This prophetic mandate continues today, and there is no shortage of ungodly rulers to confront. A single person with social or political power can inspire movements and produce countless moments needing responses. O. Wesley Allen Jr. addresses this daunting task in *Preaching in the Era of Trump*. After the election of Donald Trump as the forty-fifth president of the United States, the question of how to present God's good news in light of a president who personified bigotry and unchecked narcissism was constant. Preaching during Trump's term was particularly challenging because the former president manipulated the media by employing various tactics of distraction and intentional controversy to control the narrative. Sundays continued to come once a week, while Trump's Twitter account was constantly active before it was suspended. Allen offers homiletic strategies to address four specific topics that arose during the Trump presidency: racism, sexism, LGBTQ+ issues, and Islamophobia.

On Racism

Allen offers four homiletic strategies for addressing racism in sermons during the Trump era. He makes clear that as a white preacher he does not have "the experience, expertise, or right to offer specific homiletical strategies for preaching in Black, Hispanic, or Asian congregations," so the strategies offered are meant for predominantly white congregations.[27] He states, "Preaching on race, however, must not be left to congregations that are victims of racism."[28] The message on racism should be drastically different in churches where the majority represent the dominant culture that has perpetuated racism and those with its victims in the pews.

Allen's first strategy is admitting that a problem exists, and he suggests white preachers use a tone of confession acknowledging both the existence of racist structures and their own participation in them. Second, Allen suggests recognizing biblical texts that invite preachers to touch on racism. He specifically references early Jewish and Christian views of Samaritans in the Gospels and Acts and the division between Gentile and Jewish Christians in the early church among others as inviting commentary on contemporary racial oppression. Third, Allen suggests addressing issues related to structural racism when racism is not the central claim of the sermon. He says, "Bringing racism into sermons dealing with other topics will normalize the discussion a great deal."[29] The fourth and final homiletic strategy offered to respond to racism is what Allen describes as the need to "normalize race." By this, he means using people of different racial and ethnic identities than the dominant identities in the congregation for sermonic illustrations. Allen, however, cautions against tokenizing persons of color and thereby implying that whiteness is the norm (e.g., "a man" versus "an African American Man").

On Sexism

On sexism, Allen offers seven homiletic strategies. The first is "to raise, honestly and explicitly, the issue of patriarchy in the world as something that is of concern to God and the church."[30] The second that Allen refers to as an "obvious strategy is 'the use of inclusive language in our liturgical and theological talk.'"[31] Third, he suggests that, in dealing with sexism, it is essential to distinguish between "sex" and "gender." Although the terms are often used synonymously, Allen states, "as technical terms 'sex' refers to biological differences (chromosomes, genitalia, hormones, etc.) and 'gender' refers to the way cultures assign certain roles and characteristics (feminine versus masculine) to different sexes." In his view, the problem of patriarchy, sexism, and misogyny is with gender, not sex.[32] Fourth, Allen suggests lifting up female leaders in the church and the world as an act of affirming the priesthood of all believers.

The fifth strategy is for congregations to see women performing the same liturgical functions as men. In this strategy, the mere act of being a woman while preaching is in itself a homiletic strategy to combat patriarchy. Combating sexism is impossible if the congregational polity is inherently sexist. This includes complementarian theology that excludes women from ministry. Some Christians are tolerant of patriarchy and misogyny from the former president because their local church assemblies model it and present it as scriptural. This view may also have contributed to Trump's election in the first place. If one's theology excludes women from leadership in the church, a woman (Hillary Clinton) leading the nation would likely have been viewed negatively as well. This is reflected in Allen's sixth homiletic strategy, which is

> to lift up women who represent a wide variety of roles in society, while avoiding only using imagery of women in roles that reinforce stereotypes: mothers, wives, nurses, teachers, housewives, and secretaries. Those images are fine—when mixed with images of men in similar familial and professional roles and with images of women in a range of other roles—doctor, businesswoman, engineer, probation officer, graduate student, mayor, clergy, and so forth.[33]

Finally, Allen's seventh homiletic strategy to address sexism is "to deal with the presentation of women in the Bible. Preachers must be honest that, as a set of ancient texts, the Christian Bible (including both testaments) is patriarchal in its outlook. One can love scripture and still be honest about problems in it. Indeed, such love requires honesty."[34] A complementarian view of women's role in the church is a direct extension of the patriarchy and misogyny that are inherent in the biblical text. While many justify limiting women through Scripture, it is important to differentiate the voice of God from the cultural setting of the text. As a strategy against sexism in broader society, it is imperative to teach the biblical and theological merits of egalitarianism from the pulpit.

On LGBTQ+ Issues

On LGBTQ+ issues, Allen offers five homiletic strategies. First, he suggests that "preachers . . . help hetero-majority congregations understand the terminology used in discussing sexual orientation and gender identity."[35] Allen suggests broadening the vocabulary of the congregation works to elevate the conversation around the related issues. Second, Allen suggests that preachers directly "address the passages that seem to deal with homosexuality."[36] He argues that the texts typically associated with same-sex relations are often taken outside of their sociohistorical context and used as proof texts. Third, Allen suggests the preacher "draw on contemporary reason and experience as theological authorities over against scripture and tradition when dealing with these matters."[37] Fourth, Allen suggests using the experiences of LGBTQ+ people in sermon imagery about topics unrelated to sexuality and gender to normalize them for straight, cisgender hearers. The fifth homiletic strategy that Allen suggests related to LGBTQ+ issues is to talk about sexual ethics frankly. This final broad strategy is aimed at preachers who seem to mention sex only in relation to homosexuality.[38]

While Allen's strategies are well suited for his context, they come from a theological position that is affirming of same-sex relationships. As the issue of same-sex relations is a lightning rod in politics, it is even more so in many churches. Several denominations have split over the issue of same-sex marriage, and others are in turmoil now. Pastors who hold a more conservative view of human sexual relations or Scripture itself are unlikely to be receptive to Allen's strategies. The third strategy of using reason and experience as authorities "over and against Scripture," for instance, is a non-starter for those who hold Scripture as the final authority on all matters. Because of this, I find Allen's strategies less than helpful in bridging the gap of polarization that is indicative of the Trump era.

Many of Trump's evangelical base justify their support for him based primarily on this issue, along with reproductive rights as the other hot-button topic. Many have been willing to tolerate racism, sexism, xenophobia, and the policies that support them if they are appeased on these two issues. For evangelicals (both the white ones who largely voted for Trump and the Black ones who didn't), a biblical argument cannot be met with one of reason and experience. There is a hermeneutic hierarchy that begins and ends with Scripture. To bridge the divide, I suggest leaning more into Allen's second strategy of directly addressing Scripture passages that deal with human sexuality. I for one believe a biblical argument can be made for affirming same-sex relationships, but this is not the path Allen (or many other affirming scholars) take. Because of this, conversations happen in silos and theological assumptions go unchallenged.

In these polarized times, preachers and by extension congregations are needed who can listen and respectfully converse about divisive topics. Healthy dialogue is a path to understanding if not agreement. The most important homiletic strategy on this issue should be to consistently speak out against hatred and challenge those who try to justify it. Hatred often hides behind theological convictions, and religious beliefs have been the cause of many atrocities against humanity. This climate requires courage to speak up for love, respect, and ethical treatment of LGBTQ+ persons—especially in more conservative circles. Regardless of personal theological views on human sexuality, feelings of hatred and dehumanization have no place in the pulpit or the life of a Christian.

On Islamophobia

McMickle and Allen both address racism (Selma), sexism (Seneca Falls), and LGBTQ+ issues (Stonewall) as issues crucial to the current era. While McMickle places his final emphasis on environmental concerns (Standing Rock), Allen focuses on Islamophobia. Like his strategy of "admitting that there is a problem" as related to racism, Allen's first homiletic strategy in addressing Islamophobia is one of confession. Specifically, Allen suggests confessing to buying into negative stereotypes based on fringe elements at the expense of 20 percent of the world's population. Naming this bias is crucial in addressing the resulting ideologies. The second strategy that Allen presents is "to help congregations actually understand something of the character, belief, and practices of Islam."[39] He breaks this strategy down into three steps: help Christians develop a more respectful view of other religions in general, develop an added appreciation specifically for the other Abrahamic religions, and find ways to teach the congregation about some of the basics of Islam. The goal of these teachings is not to promote Islam or any other faith but to remove the stigma we assign to it in the spirit of loving our neighbor.

Pastor First, Prophet Second

While using different phraseology McMickle, Gilbert, LaRue, and Allen effectively make the same argument: the pastoral voice should be used frequently and the prophetic voice when necessary. McMickle suggests pastors not confront Pharaoh every Sunday. Gilbert emphasizes the importance of the priestly and sagely voices. LaRue contrasts domains of experience, and Allen says, "The order should almost always be a movement from pastor to prophet instead of the other way around."[40] He argues that strong pastoral relationships undergird the prophetic voice even when congregants disagree with the stance on the issue addressed. Prophets by nature are not popular, but the pastor's task is to speak prophetic truths in a manner that will be received by the people. As Allen repeats, "It is not the preacher's job simply to preach the gospel; it is the preacher's job to get the gospel heard, then believed, and then lived."[41]

Preaching with Moral Imagination

In *How to Preach a Dangerous Sermon*, Frank A. Thomas distinguishes between what is political and what is moral. He suggests preachers should have the courage to preach the moral base of issues, and this may lead to accusations of preaching politics. Thomas calls such preaching "dangerous sermons."[42] Preaching about universal healthcare, environmental issues, or addressing white supremacy and white privilege can be dangerous sermons. Each coincides with polarized political views. Nevertheless, they represent moral issues that should be addressed through relevant preaching. Thomas laments the lack of moral imagination in much contemporary preaching. In the words of William Barber, "Cute, cuddly preaching that does not trouble or take the risk of the gospel is theological malpractice at best, heresy at worst."[43] Still, balance is necessary for the tone and content of preaching, as with McMickle, Gilbert, LaRue, and Allen, Thomas cautions against addressing controversial issues in every sermon, but he argues, "At least some of the sermons one preaches should be dangerous."[44]

The Four Qualities of Moral Imagination
Thomas makes a case for preaching dangerous sermons using the legacies of Martin Luther King Jr. and Robert F. Kennedy as examples. Thomas draws parallels between the chaotic time of King and

Kennedy and the current social and cultural context. He rightly points out that some argue that "the time of single and solitary moral leadership is over; moral leadership is more diffused and local in its expression than one national charismatic moral leader."[45] Still, the moral leadership of the past aids in the task of moral imagination today. Whether facing the water hoses of Bull Conner or the Twitter finger of Donald Trump, the voice of moral imagination has always been necessary both in the pulpit and the public square. From the template of Kennedy's speech in Indianapolis on April 4, 1968 (the night of King's assassination), and King's "I've Been to the Mountaintop" the night before in Memphis, Thomas offers four qualities of the moral imagination.

The first quality of moral imagination that Thomas highlights in Kennedy's speech is the capacity to envision equality and represent that through his physical presence.[46] As Black communities countrywide were rioting after King's assassination, Kennedy could have canceled his appearance in a Black neighborhood of Indianapolis out of fear of repercussions and bodily harm. Instead, he showed up. By doing so at the risk of violence, he communicated the depth of his concern. Before a word was spoken, his presence illustrated moral imagination.

Second, Kennedy "saw empathy as a catalyst or bridge to create opportunities to overcome the past and make new decisions for peace and justice."[47] Kennedy harnessed King's death as an "opportunity for all to see their common humanity and create a better community."[48] He used the experience of his own brother's death by an assassin's bullet as an opportunity to show understanding and join in the grief of the community.

The third quality of moral imagination from Kennedy's speech is to "find wisdom in ancient texts, sources of ancient wisdom and truth, the wisdom of the ages."[49] Thomas points to Kennedy's crisis of faith following his brother's death, which led him to find meaning in Greek mythology. In the speech, Kennedy quotes the

Greek tragedian Aeschylus: "Even in our sleep, pain which cannot forget . . . comes wisdom through the awful grace of God."[50] In the Greek myths, Kennedy saw the dangers of human pride and arrogance. Likewise, Thomas suggests that as Kennedy found meaning in Greek mythology so the Christian preacher must communicate the wisdom of the Bible in response to chaotic times and events.

The final quality of moral imagination illustrated in Kennedy's speech is that he "addressed the audience in the language of poetry and art that lifts and elevates the human spirit by touching the emotive chords of wonder, mystery, and hope."[51] While the listeners may not have been intellectually familiar with Aeschylus, they were able to emotively feel the quote's meaning. LaRue points to creative uses of language as one of the characteristics of Black preaching. He says, "The traditional Black church expects and appreciates rhetorical flair and highly poetic language in the preaching of the gospel . . . Unlike many European and mainline American denominations, where architecture and classical music inspire a sense of the holy, Blacks seek to accomplish this act through the display of well-crafted rhetoric."[52] This is not simply a matter of flowery language as an aesthetic enhancement but the means to effectively communicate hope during turbulent times.

Sermonic Examples: Prathia Hall

"Between the Wilderness and a Cliff"
(Hampton University Ministers Conference, 1992)
Both Gilbert and Thomas point to Prathia L. Hall as an example of the moral imagination and prophetic balance necessary for preaching controversial topics. Hall was a pastor, professor, revivalist, and freedom fighter. A native of Philadelphia, she was one of the first women field leaders for the Student Nonviolent Coordinating Committee (SNCC) in southwest Georgia before returning north to pastor the Rose of Sharon Baptist Church in

Philadelphia. She attended Princeton Theological Seminary, where she received master's and doctoral degrees. She specialized in womanist theology, ethics, and African American church history. She held several faculty positions at universities, seminaries, and centers for the study of religious life. Hall was ordained in the American Baptist Church, an officer in the Progressive National Baptist Convention, and the first woman member of the Baptist Ministers' Conference of Philadelphia and Vicinity. In 1997, she was featured by *Ebony* magazine as one of the outstanding African American woman preachers in America.[53] Whether responding to patriarchy and misogyny in the media, in the workforce, from the president of the United States, or in the local church, sexism is an ever-present current event for women preachers. Hall was vocal and prolific in her advocacy for women (and fellow women preachers in particular), but she never limited her preaching voice to prophetically calling out the constant injustices. She exemplified Thomas's moral imagination while maintaining the balance of preaching voice shown in Gilbert's trivocal approach and LaRue's domains of experience.

Gilbert uses excerpts from Hall's sermon "Between the Wilderness and the Cliff" to illustrate her trivocal preaching voice.[54] The sermon is based on Luke 4:14-15, 20, and 28-30 and is one of Hall's best-known. It was featured in several publications and preached in several high-profile pulpits, including the Hampton University Ministers' Conference. By drawing on her personal experiences and the wisdom of the ancient text, Hall clearly illustrates Thomas's moral imagination and its role in preaching. Notably, she says, "If what we do in the pulpit is not good news to the poor, deliverance to the captives, sight to the blind, healing from the broken, and freedom for the oppressed, it may be sweet, it may be eloquent, it may even be deep, but it ain't preaching."[55]

Gilbert highlights excerpts from "Between the Wilderness and the Cliff" that fit each of the three voices of trivocal preaching. He highlights Hall's prophetic voice when she says, "My sisters and brothers, a surrendered identity is deadly. It is more deadly than lost identity. Surrendered identity means that you intentionally relinquish who you are, and you voluntarily sell out God's divine ministry."[56] Here, she speaks to women who have been silenced and marginalized and calls out the ones who have limited them. The priestly voice is shown when Hall says, "So preachers, teachers, servants of God, don't you get tangled up between the wilderness and the cliff. Don't you surrender your identity. Sister preacher, whether they believe you or not, you [sic] better know who you are."[57] More than highlighting the oppression and calling out the oppressor, the priestly voice affirms the identity of the marginalized calling her to hope and perseverance. Finally, in the sagely voice, Hall says, "My friends, the context of our ministries is between the wilderness and the cliff, but we are able to escape the crowd. He escaped through their midst. We escape the people, but only through the very people who would hurl us over the cliff, for these are the people whom God has called us to serve."[58] In this excerpt, she communicates the wisdom of the ages reminding the listener that escape is possible but not without struggle. In highlighting Satan's temptation of Jesus, she says, "That's the deal. Prizes without pain."[59] The sagely voice calls to remembrance the struggles and victories of the past for hope in the present.

"Freedom Faith" (Brown Chapel AME Church, Selma, Alabama, March 23, 2000)

In *How to Preach a Dangerous Sermon*, Thomas says Hall "leaves a giant testimony of moral imagination."[60] He draws comparisons between his "moral imagination" and what Hall termed "freedom faith." Thomas says, "Hall first coined the phrase, freedom faith, in 1997, but described it as early as 1965 as she witnessed the courage and resilience of local Black residents and their supporters in the Deep South in their fight against racial oppression."[61] Freedom faith, as a concept, was developed directly in response to the context of the struggle of these residents and supporters. Thomas says, "Hall believed that these freedom fighters' ability to blend their longing for social, political, and economic freedom with their Christian faith was the spiritual force that kept them in the struggle."[62] This is the heart of moral imagination and the driving force behind effective current-event preaching.

Thomas shows each of the four qualities of the moral imagination in the definition of freedom faith. First, by participating in marches, protests, boycotts, and so on, Hall represented the envisioned equality through her physical presence. Second, Thomas says, "She saw empathy, sacrifice, and death as a catalyst or bridge to create opportunities to overcome the past and make new decisions for peace and justice."[63] Third, Hall used the wisdom of the ancient text, particularly the Bible, evidenced by her expository preaching. Finally, Hall used "the language of poetry and art that lifts and elevates and creates wonder, mystery, and hope in the hearts of people" evidenced by her skillful oration in preaching the gospel.

Hall exemplified "freedom faith." In the sermon of the same name, she used Galatians 5:1, 13-14 as grounding Scripture. The setting for the sermon was the Brown Chapel AME Church in Selma, Alabama. Some thirty-five years after the events of what has become known as "Bloody Sunday" in Selma, Hall recounted her experiences of that day. She recounted the events on the Edmond Pettus Bridge, comparing their anguish with that of Jesus on Calvary. After detailing the events of Bloody Sunday and the drive to freedom through faith that pushed the protesters on that day, she turned her focus to the present saying, "The scripture does not allow us to rest upon the Freedom Faith of our foremothers and forefathers. It has a compelling word to us right now. Indeed, it has a word for us as we march into the twenty-first century."[64] Here, Hall recontextualized from a sagely remembrance to a prophetic call to current action.

Although not technically a current event since the sermon was preached thirty-five years after the events of Bloody Sunday in 1965, the content of "Freedom Faith" is nevertheless driven as a response to the events of that day. Furthermore, the citizens of Selma and the nation remain disturbed by the images from that day. She addressed a congregation in Selma regarding the events that inspired McMickle's use of Selma as a category of social concern in preaching. But rather than dwelling on the historic events, she addressed the continued concerns of the gathered community. While issuing a clear call to prophetic action, she maintained the empathetic tone of pastor/priest. The life and ministry of Prathia Hall exemplify the crucial need for both bravery and balance in relevant preaching in response to current events or, in this case, current contexts considering historic events.

In recent years, a new brand of freedom faith has emerged. As the events in Selma on Bloody Sunday galvanized a generation of preachers and activists to address the racism of the Jim Crow South, so a series of high-profile deaths of unarmed Black Americans at the hands of law enforcement and rogue civilians has now galvanized a new generation to engage and employ moral imagination. Next, we will examine the Black Lives Matter (BLM) movement and the preaching it has produced, beginning with the death of Trayvon Martin at the hands of neighborhood watchman George Zimmerman in Sanford, Florida, and Zimmerman's subsequent acquittal.

Reflection Questions before You Preach

1. What are the potential consequences if I address this moment?

2. What is at stake if I don't address this moment?

3. Does this moment require *parrhesia*? (bold speech without regard for the speaker's safety)

4. Is this a moment for prophetic correction, or would the voice of the priest or sage be more appropriate?

5. Have I developed strong enough pastoral relationships to impact those who may disagree?

Notes

1. Marvin A. McMickle, *The Making of a Preacher: Five Essentials for Today's Ministers* (Valley Forge, PA: Judson Press, 2018).

2. Ibid., 85.

3. Paul Tillich, quoted in Karl Barth, *The Preaching of the Gospel* (Philadelphia: Westminster Press, 1963), 54.

4. McMickle, 123.

5. Ibid., 120, quoting Paul Lehman.

6. Ibid., 132.

7. Ibid., 86.

8. Cornell West, *Black Prophetic Fire* (Boston: Beacon Press, 2014).

9. Barack Obama, "Second Inaugural Address," US presidential inauguration, Washington, DC, January 20, 2013.

10. McMickle, 111.

11. Ibid., 85.

12. Kenyatta Gilbert, *The Journey and Promise of African American Preaching* (Minneapolis: Fortress Press, 2011), 89.

13. Ibid., 90.

14. Ibid., 91.

15. Ibid.

16. Ibid., 14.

17. Cleophas J. LaRue, *The Heart of Black Preaching* (Louisville, KY: Westminster John Knox, 2000), 20.

18. Ibid.
19. Ibid., 21.
20. Ibid., 22.
21. Ibid., 23.
22. Ibid.
23. Ibid.
24. Ibid., 24.
25. Ibid.
26. Ibid., 1.
27. O. Wesley Allen Jr., *Preaching in the Era of Trump* (Danvers, MA: Chalice Press, 2017).
28. Ibid., 50.
29. Ibid., 65.
30. Ibid.
31. Ibid., 67.
32. Ibid., 68.
33. Ibid., 79.
34. Ibid.
35. Ibid., 92.
36. Ibid., 93.
37. Ibid., 103.
38. Ibid., 24.
39. Ibid.
40. Ibid.
41. Ibid., 27.
42. Frank A. Thomas, *How to Preach a Dangerous Sermon* (Nashville: Abingdon, 2018), 89.
43. Ibid., 106, quoting William Barber.
44. Ibid., introduction.
45. Ibid., 75.
46. Ibid., foreword.
47. Ibid., 53.
48. Ibid., 73.
49. Ibid., 17.
50. Ibid., 18.

51. Ibid.

52. LaRue, 10.

53. *Ebony*, November 1997.

54. Gilbert, 113.

55. Ibid.

56. Ibid.

57. Ibid.

58. Ibid.

59. Ibid.

60. Thomas, preface.

61. Ibid.

62. Ibid., 105.

63. Ibid., 106.

64. Ibid., 109.

CHAPTER 4

July 14, 2013

The Moment That Birthed the Movement

Every generation faces events that test what Prathia Hall called freedom faith and require the use of what Frank Thomas frames as moral imagination. In recent years, several public instances of police and civilian violence against Black Americans have galvanized those with moral imagination to use their voices for proclamation and their feet for action. These instances of violence, the lack of favorable court decisions, and the resulting protests and civil unrest have occupied the news cycle and the minds of many Black Americans, as well as others who are justice-minded, for roughly the last seven years. Specific events which garnered national attention and may have precipitated sermonic response include the police shooting of Michael Brown and the resulting protests in Ferguson, Missouri; the police shooting of twelve-year-old Tamir Rice in Cleveland, Ohio; the police-involved death by asphyxiation of Eric Garner in Staten Island, New York; and the death of Sandra Bland while in police custody in Waller County, Texas, among many others.

Origins of Black Lives Matter

Of particular significance is the shooting death of seventeen-year-old Trayvon Martin in Sanford, Florida, at the hands of George Zimmerman, followed by a not guilty verdict in Zimmerman's trial. The murder of Martin and Zimmerman's subsequent acquittal largely precipitated the increased focus on unjust killings of Black Americans at the hands of law enforcement. In response to Zimmerman's acquittal, three self-described "radical Black organizers," Alicia Garza, Patrisse Cullors, and Opal Tometi, started what has become known as the #BlackLivesMatter movement. Movement organizers describe BLM as "an ideological and political intervention in a world where Black lives are systematically and intentionally targeted for demise. It is an affirmation of Black folks' humanity, our contributions to this society, and our resilience in the face of deadly oppression."[1] Officially, BLM is a loosely connected global network of more than forty local chapters working to organize and intervene in instances of violence against Black people. Beyond that, the phrase "Black Lives Matter" has become a rallying cry for liberation in the face of unjust state-sanctioned murder.

Besides being a response to the unjust killing of Black people, Black Lives Matter as an organization also responds to the internal marginalization that has existed within previous Black liberation movements. The BLM website says, "Black liberation movements in this country have created room, space, and leadership mostly for Black heterosexual, cisgender men—leaving women, queer and transgender people, and others either out of the movement or in the background to move the work forward with little or no recognition."[2] Within the DNA of the BLM movement as organized by Garza, Cullors, and Tometi is the commitment to be "intentional about not replicating harmful practices that excluded so many in past movements for liberation, we made a commitment to placing those at the margins closer to the center."[3]

The notion of past liberation movements themselves being instruments of marginalization can be read as an indictment on the Black church. BLM as a secular movement is in many ways a response to the inadequacies and blind spots of previous movements centered on Black religious identity. The "Herstory" section of the official Black Lives Matter website says, "Black liberation movements in this country have created room, space, and leadership mostly for Black heterosexual, cisgender men—leaving women, queer and transgender people, and others either out of the movement or in the background to move the work forward with little or no recognition."[4] While the Black church has long been a voice on issues of race, it has simultaneously been silent or complicit on issues of gender, sexual orientation, and gender identity. To paraphrase McMickle, the church has addressed "Selma" while ignoring "Seneca Falls" and "Stonewall."[5] To view state-sanctioned violence against Blacks as simply a racial issue is to miss the key intersections that BLM seeks to address. The fight for justice and equality has shifted from the "I am a man" racial patriarchy of the civil rights movement to the more complex layers of gender, sex, and sexuality. As this shift has happened, many in the new generation of activists view the church with a hermeneutic of suspicion because of the role of religion in the castigation of LGBTQ+ and women.

Secular Organization, Spiritual Movement

The focus on intersectionality within the BLM movement is an example of the secularization of activism in the twenty-first century. However, while BLM has become the face of the fight against state-sanctioned violence against Blacks, the voice of the Black preacher has certainly not been silent. To truly understand church involvement, "Black Lives Matter" the organization must be separated from "Black Lives Matter" the movement. The church may not be leading the organization known as BLM, but many of the larger movement's voices are rooted in the Black church's legacy of activism. When the movement is separated from the organization, the notion of secularized activism in the twenty-first century appears largely overstated. Both locally and nationally, lay members and clergy engage in the work of organizing. Church bodies are comforting and counseling the families of the lost, and pastors are preaching relevant messages that combat residual trauma and mobilize church members to do the work of justice. Many voices in pulpits across America have willingly participated in the movement for Black lives. These sermonic voices have arisen in response to the same series of events in public culture and share the same starting point—the murder of Trayvon Martin and the acquittal of George Zimmerman.

In *Rest in Power*, a memoir written by Trayvon Martin's parents about the death of their son and the subsequent birth of the Black Lives Matter movement, it is clear that faith and the Black church were central to that movement. Many who supported the family were Black clergy. Names associated with the fight for justice in the case of Trayvon Martin include Rev. Al Sharpton, Rev. Jamal Bryant, Rev. Ludence Robinson, Rev. Arthur Jackson III, Bishop Victor Curry, Reverend Gaston E. Smith, Pastor Walter Richardson, and Reverend Gregory Williams, among others.[6] Whether increasing media attention or providing direct support to Sybrina Fulton and Tracy Martin, each of these preachers was mentioned by name for their work in the aftermath of Trayvon's death. Even Benjamin Crump, the civil rights attorney who represented the family, rooted his practice on the strong foundation of faith and the moral imperative to pursue justice. According to Tracy Martin, during the height of his anger over his son's death, Crump whispered in his ear, "God is in control, and we don't need to help God. God is going to make sure that this wrong is made right; we don't have to do anything more at this point."[7] This exemplifies what Prathia Hall referred to as "freedom faith" and would prove to be a theme during the ordeal which birthed the movement.

Sybrina Fulton's (Trayvon's mother) faith was particularly pronounced. Fulton presents herself as a Christian of deep conviction.

She is a faithful member of the Antioch Baptist Church of Miami Gardens, attending Sunday school at 9:30 and service at 11:00 a.m. Her favorite Bible passage, Proverbs 3:5-6, guided her during the devastation of losing her son and the tumultuous media frenzy and trial that followed. Her faith guided her through it all and still does today. Even in the aftermath of the Zimmerman acquittal, Fulton's faith was on display as she tweeted, "Lord during my darkest hour I lean on you. You are all that I have. At the end of the day, GOD is still in control. Thank you all for your prayers and support. I will love you forever Trayvon!!! In the name of Jesus!!!"[8] Likewise, after the trial Trayvon's father, Tracy Martin, tweeted, "Even though I am broken hearted my faith is unshattered I WILL ALWAYS LOVE MY BABY TRAY." These were people of faith in need of spiritual encouragement, as were so many others who empathized with their plight.

The Preaching Moment, Sunday, July 14, 2013

Nearly seventeen months after Trayvon Martin's death, on Saturday, July 13, 2013, a jury rendered a verdict of not guilty on all counts in the case of the state of Florida v. George Zimmerman after sixteen hours of deliberation. The timing of Zimmerman's acquittal was particularly challenging to those with Sunday preaching assignments because the verdict was publicly announced at roughly 10:00 p.m. on Saturday, July 13, 2013. While the notion of a "Saturday night special" is an often-maligned colloquialism for sermons haphazardly thrown together, the truth is that a sermon prepared on Saturday night is sometimes necessitated by the events of Saturday evening. In situations like this, a full night's sleep becomes a sacrifice for the cause of the gospel.

That fateful Saturday night was more than a singular event—it was the culmination of nearly a year and a half of anger, protest, racism, conjecture, and Internet opining. Skittles candy and

Arizona iced tea had already become symbols of resistance based on what Trayvon had purchased from the store that night. President Barack Obama weighed in, noting that "if I had a son, he'd look like Trayvon,"[10] along with a chorus of talking heads and social pundits. The same preachers praying about how to respond to this verdict had already preached in hoodies as an act of solidarity months before, but this moment was different. After the verdict, there was tension, uncertainty, and despair. There were memories of the Rodney King verdict in 1992 and questions of whether the riots would be nationwide this time. Cities across the country braced themselves for the response to what many viewed as an egregious breach of justice. Pastors in communities still in shambles from the riots of previous generations wondered if history would repeat itself. There was no way to pretend this didn't happen—the verdict that Black America held their collective breaths waiting on was rendered, and it was the worst-case scenario. A situation like this meant whatever sermon or series had been prepared needed to be modified or rewritten to address the weight of concern in the minds and hearts of the congregation.

Lizette Alvarez and Cara Buckley documented the scene at the courthouse after the verdict for the *New York Times* stating, "Outside the courthouse, perhaps a hundred protesters who had been gathering through the night, their numbers building as the hours passed, began pumping their fists in the air, waving placards and chanting 'No justice, no peace!'" However, by an hour after the verdict was read the crowd had dissipated; "fists were no longer aloft, placards had come down."[11] There was no riot on the courtroom steps—only the despair of facing the reality that, despite the public outcry, justice was not served in this case. However, as the voice of the crowd on the courtroom steps grew silent, the distraught voice of discontent grew to deafening portions on social media. The wildfire speed of the Internet age meant the verdict and the discussion thereof had instantly gone viral. The anger of those emotionally affected was palpable. Family attorney Benjamin Crump "urged Mr. Martin's parents to stay out of the courtroom for the verdict. They were home and planning to attend church on Sunday."[12] Like many others in this time of confusion, anger, and despair, Trayvon's family sought the comfort of Christian fellowship and a word from God relevant to their situation.

Rev. Dr. Leslie Callahan, "Neighborhood Watch" (St. Paul's Baptist Church, Philadelphia)

On Sunday, July 14, 2013, Dr. Leslie D. Callahan, pastor of the St. Paul's Baptist Church in Philadelphia, preached a sermon titled "Neighborhood Watch" from Luke 10:25-37, which was in the common lectionary readings for that day. She subsequently preached another version of the same sermon the next day at the Samuel DeWitt Proctor Institute for Child Advocacy's Children's Defense Fund (CDF) held at the CDF Haley Farm in Clinton, Tennessee. The message builds upon the irony of George Zimmerman's role as a Neighborhood Watch volunteer. Quoting the Neighborhood Watch website, Callahan states, "Not only does Neighborhood Watch allow citizens to help in the fight against crime, it is also an opportunity for communities to bond, through service. The Neighborhood Watch Program draws upon the compassion of average citizens, asking them to lend their neighbors a hand."[13] Compassion, service, community bonding, and lending neighbors a hand sound like bedrock Christian principles as if they were directly adapted from Jesus's great commandment to "love your neighbor as yourself."

Sadly, these principles did not play out in the manner intended on the night that Trayvon was killed. Callahan diagnoses the disconnect between the mission of Neighborhood Watch and the action of Zimmerman that night. "The problem is that George Zimmerman, when he asked himself the question, 'Who is my neighbor?' did not include Trayvon Martin. He *was* his neighbor;

he just never even gave it any consideration that it was possible."[14] This disconnect frames the sermon's theme and challenges the listeners with two overarching questions: who is my neighbor? and its unspoken corollary, who is not my neighbor? These pointed and challenging questions build upon the conversation between Jesus and an expert in the law and the parable of the Good Samaritan. Callahan masterfully approaches both the precipitating conversation and the parable itself in the quest to answer the pertinent questions.

The question who is my neighbor? was posed in the text by an expert in Jewish law. This interchange in Luke 10 began with the lawyer asking Jesus a simpler question: "What must I do to inherit eternal life?" The lawyer knew that the answer to his first question was "Love the Lord your God with all your heart and with all your soul and with all your strength and with all your mind," and "Love your neighbor as yourself." However, Callahan suggests that the lawyer was searching for a loophole when he asked the additional question, "But who is my neighbor?" While the lawyer's motivation for asking the question was dubious, it is nevertheless one that is necessary to ask. The spirit of "love your neighbor as yourself" is compromised because of the implicit unspoken question, "Who is my neighbor?" Callahan poses a series of rapid-fire hypothetical questions in the voice of the lawyer in the text:

> "How much loving of the neighbor do I have to do?"
>
> "How far do I have to go before I'm outside of the bounds of the neighborhood?"
>
> "How far do I have to reach before my love can run out?"
>
> "Who is it that I have to love like myself?"
>
> "Who is it that I can leave by the wayside and forget that they even exist?"
>
> "Who is it who is my neighbor, and who can I treat like they're not even human?"

These questions not only build upon the loophole-seeking lawyer in Luke 10 but also expose how each of us seeks loopholes in the fulfilling of God's commandment to love our neighbor. This nation has a long history of deciding who is and who isn't worthy of being considered a neighbor. Callahan quotes Richard Wright in his 1937 essay "The Ethics of Living Jim Crow" to illustrate this principle at work in the segregated South:

> Negros who live south know the dread of being caught alone upon the streets of white neighborhoods after the sun has set. In such a simple situation as this, the plight of the negro in America is graphically symbolized. While white strangers may be in these neighborhoods trying to get home, they can pass unmolested, but the color of a negro's skin makes him easily recognizable, makes him suspect, converts him into a defenseless target.[15]

This making of a suspect and being a "defenseless target" would be bad enough if confined to a tale of the 1930s Jim Crow South. But the murder of Trayvon Martin in 2012 and the acquittal of his killer a year later show that Richard Wright's account is sadly still accurate in the twenty-first century.

Remarkably, Callahan resists the urge to preach to the choir in her sermon. It would be easy to opine on the so-called criminal injustice system and rail against the George Zimmermans of the world, stoking the anger and self-righteousness of the listening audience. Instead, she takes the opportunity to challenge those to whom she was preaching to not make the same mistakes:

> I'm not George Zimmerman's pastor; he never called me and asked me to say a word to him, I'm not talking to George Zimmerman. I'm talking to folks who gathered at Hailey Farm, because we believe in a wide neighborhood.

> But I'm wondering: can you admit, that as wide as you
> believe the neighborhood ought to be, there are some folks
> that you don't think of as your neighbor, some people
> you'd like to leave out of your neighborhood?[16]

These challenging words illustrate how the "othering" of people
who should be our neighbors is unique neither to George
Zimmerman nor the lawyer in Luke 10 nor the priest and Levite
of the parable. The structural failure in the murder of Trayvon and
the acquittal of George Zimmerman is an opportunity for all of us
to examine ourselves.

In Luke 10, Jesus responds to the lawyer's query with what is
known as the parable of the Good Samaritan. In the parable, a
man was traveling from Jerusalem to Jericho when he was attacked
by robbers, stripped of his clothes, and beaten half to death. A
priest and a Levite both passed to the other side of the road upon
seeing the injured man, but a Samaritan took pity on him. The
Samaritan bandaged the injured man's wounds with oil and wine,
put the man on his own donkey, and brought him to an inn. Then,
the Samaritan paid the innkeeper to care for the injured man.
Callahan builds drama around the actions of the priest and the
Levite highlighting their lack of compassion:

> I imagine the Levite and the priest got to the prayer meet-
> ing because they were giving their testimony about how
> the Lord brought them through dangers seen and unseen.
> You know, church, I was on the Jericho Road today, and
> you know how dangerous the Jericho Road is. It was so
> dangerous that there was a man lying there. I thank God I
> didn't come ten minutes earlier; it could have been me![17]

This exercise in sanctified imagination illustrates how our own self-
ish testimonies can violate the principle of loving our neighbor as

ourselves and how people of faith today can fit the mold of the priest and Levite in the text.

Callahan also reminds the audience of the irony of the Samaritan being the rescuer. Samaritan meant "somebody who got God wrong. Not only were they ethnically impure, but they were theologically incorrect."[18] The Samaritans were the "other." The Samaritans were the ones who didn't qualify as a neighbor, but in this parable, the Samaritan showed righteousness far greater than the religious elites who crossed to the other side of the road. In Callahan's words, "While the priest had a Bible, and the Levite a hymn book, the Samaritan had a heart."[19] Beyond lamenting the injustice of Zimmerman's acquittal, Callahan calls on her listening audience to see everyone as their neighbor and avoid the "othering" that led to Trayvon's death.

Dr. Roger L. Ray, "Trayvon Is Dead and None of Us Are 'Not Guilty'" (The Emerging Church, Springfield, Missouri)
Like Dr. Callahan, Dr. Roger L. Ray preached from the lectionary text in Luke 10 in a sermon titled "Trayvon Is Dead and None of Us Are 'Not Guilty.'" Unlike Dr. Callahan (a Black woman), Dr. Ray is a white man, which is significant. Since the Trayvon Martin shooting and the subsequent not guilty verdict are largely viewed as Black issues affecting the Black community, a white man addressing this topic in a full sermon the morning after the verdict is noteworthy. Black pastors addressing Black issues before Black congregations are an important part of our cultural expression and crucial for solidarity amid numerous traumatic circumstances. But for real progress, white congregations must address these issues as well. Hearing a fresh take on the verdict from a white male pastor provides a different lens and speaks to a different audience, arguably the audience that needs to hear it the most. Ray is the pastor of the Emerging Church in Springfield, Missouri (formerly known as Community Christian

Church). The Emerging Church self-describes as "a progressive interfaith community."[20]

Ray spends the first half of his fourteen-minute sermon addressing the verdict and various related race and social issues. When he addresses Luke 10, he frames the text as a challenge to his mostly white congregation. He specifically targets complacency and self-righteousness among those who might consider themselves to be the good guys. In his analysis of the parable, he asks the congregation to reject any goodwill they think they gain by being progressive or socially conscious. He urges them instead to acknowledge that, despite their good works, they still may be subject to implicit racism or internal hatred. He pointedly states, "What I'm asking you to consider about this biblical parable is that the guy we call the good Samaritan may have found this beaten half-dead Jew and even though he stopped, picked him up, took him to get help, and even paid for it out of his pocket, he may very well have still hated the man and everything that he represented."[21] In an age of populist rebellion against what is called political correctness, in which many take more offense to being labeled as racist than they do actual racism, calling a mostly white congregation to reflect on their own biases is both remarkable and necessary, particularly in a group that identifies as politically and theologically progressive. While the political right and Christian fundamentalism have borne the brunt of the blame for oppressive policy and theology, the left are certainly not without sin. An outward ethic of social progress does not always change the internal biases that have been embedded over generations.

The simple and ironic turn of phrase, "none of us are 'not guilty,'" uses the immediacy of the verdict from the previous night but turns the attention from the inadequacies of the criminal justice system to the personal inadequacies of each individual listener. Ray further challenges the listeners: "Even if he fired in self-defense, this is not an innocent incident. There were a number of bad decisions that led up to the very sad and very wrong death of Trayvon Martin, but no one here should pretend that there's not someone out there in the world that you're afraid of, someone you distrust at the very sight of them."[22] The call to self-reflection and confession is necessary before repentance can occur.

While calling out social ills is surely part of a prophetic sermon, ultimately, the message must have relevance and application for the hearers. To call out the criminal justice system, the actions of the police in Sanford, Florida, prosecutorial overreach, the stand-your-ground law, or even George Zimmerman himself, are each part of the building of social conscience. But when calling out wrongs is not paired with a call for personal reflection, they do little to change the prevailing narrative. In this way, Dr. Ray reflects the words of Dr. Callahan, who declared, "I'm not George Zimmerman's pastor." It is imperative when preaching through current events to consider the audience one is preaching to and speak directly to their needs. When racial injustice is committed upon a Black teenager, color blindness serves no one. The needs of a Black church audience, a white one, a mixed congregation, or those of other cultures are all different, but the need for self-reflection remains for all.

In the 1906 satirical book *Observation by Mr. Dooley* by Peter Finley Dunne, the fictional Dooley says in his signature broken English, "Th' newspaper does ivrything f'r us . . . comforts th' afflicted, afflicts th' comfortable."[23] This phrase has been adapted from its original satirical context and applied without jest to other settings, notably the role of God and the preachers who stand in God's stead. To "comfort the afflicted" and "afflict the comfortable" accurately sums up the task of the preacher who stands after a major social, political, or cultural event. The challenge is to determine which category the listening congregation falls in. On July 14, 2013, Dr. Ray determined that the congregation at the Emerging Church in Springfield fit into the latter.

Rev. Dr. Howard-John Wesley, "When the Verdict Hurts" (Alfred Street Baptist Church, Alexandria, Virginia)

Unlike Ray, Dr. Howard-John Wesley saw his task at the Alfred Street Baptist Church in Alexandria, Virginia, as comforting the afflicted, even as he himself needed comforting. As Ray preached through the lens of a socially conscious white man, Wesley preached from the callused perspective of a hurt Black man. For Wesley, this was not a mere exercise in social commentary for a spiritual end. This was a deeply personal and traumatic event that he struggled to address. From the opening salutations, he was visibly affected by the verdict and the cumulative effects of the murder and trial over the previous seventeen months. The sermon, entitled "When the Verdict Hurts," was a raw emotional lament that called the congregation at Alfred Street to collective mourning but left them with the hope necessary to carry on. *Time* contributor Elizabeth Dias described the message as "the best sermon about Trayvon that you will hear," stating in the article of the same name, "If you hear one sermon about America's Trayvon Martin moment, let it be this one."[24] Wesley's platform at the historic Alfred Street Baptist Church and his proximity to Washington, DC, the epicenter of national policy, caused his words to have a particularly strong effect on the consciousness of the nation.

Dr. Wesley opens the sermon by discussing his decision to depart from his teaching series ironically titled "Survivor Mode." Regarding the paused preaching series, he states:

> I preached part 2 of that message last night at our 6:00 p.m. service. We looked at the woman with the issue of blood and how it is she's able to survive. I think the sermon went all right, the choir seemed to like it, some folks shouted, and a few folks joined. And it was my intent to continue that series and that sermon on this morning with

you. Went home last night after church feeling pretty good, and all that changed about twelve hours ago.[25]

Wesley describes the moment and the decision that so many pastors faced that same night, the emotional turbulence of the moment, and the determination of how to address it with the Sunday preaching moment at hand. He lays out his decision by bringing the congregation into his process as a moment of transparency. "It just didn't seem that it was appropriate to continue business as usual in this sermon today. God was pressing and pushing something different that we need to speak in this moment, and I ask for your prayers as what I bring has just been prayerfully shaped overnight. We're trusting that it's what God wants to speak."[26] While sermons and sermon series ideally take time to craft, occasions like these necessity messages are "prayerfully shaped overnight." This is never a pleasant experience for the pastor who has worked all week on another message, and the decision to change course is one not taken lightly. With his honest introduction, Wesley gives the congregation a window into the discomfort of his process, inviting them to be active participants.

Wesley's text came from Mark 15:21: "Then they compelled a certain man, Simon a Cyrenian, the father of Alexander and Rufus, as he was coming out of the country and passing by, to bear his [Jesus's] cross." Simon is presented as one literally carrying the weight of Jesus's unjust verdict, the way the Black community found themselves figuratively carrying the weight of the Zimmerman verdict. The relevance of this text is accentuated by the African identity of Simon. Wesley called upon the African roots of his historically Black church to connect their plight with that of Simon. In the tradition of Black prophetic preaching, Wesley is unapologetic in his playing of the proverbial race card. As Black preachers and indeed for every Black person, we have no choice but to play the cards we have been dealt.

As Cleophas LaRue illustrates in his corporate concerns domain of experience, the space of Black churches allows us to address these instances of community trauma within the safety of fellowship.[27] Wesley describes this preaching through the lens of race as "racial consciousness." Not a lot of multicultural spaces allow African Americans or other marginalized groups to honestly address and heal from trauma, so from its origins, the Black church has served this purpose as a sanctuary from the marginalization and oppression of life within the shadow of the dominant culture. Wesley states:

> I have a racial consciousness that lets me know that in situations like this that it typically doesn't work out in our favor. I know you can't say it. It's politically incorrect, and you can't bring it up on your job 'cause they'll send you to HR, but I can say it in this place. What would be the outcome if the color roles were reversed? If this were a young Black man that had taken a white life, would we be wrestling with it like this this morning?[28]

With these words, he publicly says what many in the congregation were already thinking. In the process of affirming the feelings of hurt, he gives voice to their questions about what's next and validates their collective fears. By validating what they were already feeling, he prepares them for the next steps of healing and action. In a powerful litany about the necessity of addressing race, he states:

> I want to take race out of it. I want to live in a world where I'm not judged by the color of my skin but the content of my character. I want to live in a world where I believe that we are created and treated equally. I want to live in a world where we're not "separate but equal" but we're unified

regardless of race or creed. But the reality is that I have to look at this through the eyes of a Black man.[29]

As a Black man, he responds from his own raw emotions. He compares Michael Vick's two-year sentence for killing an animal with Zimmerman, who killed a Black boy and walked away free. As a Black man, he channels the generations of mistreatment of Black boys and Black men that have precipitated this moment after the verdict. As a Black man and a Black father, he considers the plight of his own Black children and what it means to live in a world where Trayvon is murdered, and his killer is acquitted. And as a Black preacher, he links the reality of his own plight with that of Simon of Cyrene, another man of African descent called to carry a cross that he did not ask for. Ultimately, through his own Black lens and the parallel of Simon from Cyrene, Wesley points to hope in the resurrection of Jesus Christ, the victim of the unjust verdict who gains victory for all through the power of resurrection. By doing this, Wesley invites all the wounded to partake in the power of that resurrection.

Otis Moss III, "A Word for Trayvon" (Trinity United Church of Christ, Chicago)

At the Trinity United Church of Christ in Chicago, Pastor Otis Moss III took a different approach. Rather than rewriting an entire sermon, he instead took ten minutes to read a prepared statement in light of the previous night's verdict. The statement contained many of the elements that one would expect in a sermon including a title, a grounding thematic Scripture, and a hopeful close that pointed to Jesus. So, the statement effectively filled the role of a sermon while not altering the official sermonic moment. Moss approached the pulpit clad along with other members of Trinity in a hoodie as a tribute to the attire of Trayvon at the time of his death and opened by quoting Jeremiah

31:15, "A voice is heard in Ramah, lamentation and bitter weeping. Rachel is weeping for her children; she refuses to be comforted for her children, because they are no more." He then flipped the verse to describe the Martin family in place of Rachel and her children: "A voice is heard in Sanford, Florida, lamentation and bitter weeping. The Martin family is weeping, for their child is no more. They refuse to be comforted because Trayvon is no longer with us."[30]

After this anchoring Scripture, Moss details the roller coaster of emotions experienced during the trial, as well as the layers of injustice that played out in the courtroom and the media. "For over sixteen months we mourned with the Martin family, we wept with the family, but we also witnessed a second murder that took place not in Sanford, Florida, but across the airwaves, as a little boy was assassinated by media outlets, pundits and bloggers and activists seeking to ignite the ever-present but latent fires of America's racialized imagination and past."[31] The notion of collective mourning and weeping with the family illustrates how the murder and subsequent trial captivated the nation and went from a family tragedy to a national movement of solidarity. But for Moss, this was more than a moment for community lament—it was deeply personal.

The majority of Moss's statement builds around a conversation he had with his own son the night of the Zimmerman verdict, less than twelve hours before he stood before the congregation at Trinity. "As I held my son last evening after the verdict, he said words that penetrated my soul and pierced my heart. With a slight tremble in his voice he said, 'Daddy, am I next?'"[32] As he states this, there is an audible gasp for breath in the congregation, one that I share as I watch the video recording. People of all ages were affected by the murder, the trial, and the verdict, but it is especially heartbreaking to hear the effect on this young Black man approaching Trayvon's age. Moss says, "I did my best to confront him and comfort him by asking God to give me words to calm the spirit of a twelve-year-old boy who sees himself in the face of another young boy named Trayvon Martin. We talked about this moment, about being called to conscience, not meaningless anger but a galvanizing moment to speak to the calling all people of faith have. We are called to be practitioners of love and justice."[33]

Moss then cites several examples of people who used galvanizing moments to speak love and justice. He references Emmitt Till's mother who eulogized her son, telling those in Chicago to "leave the casket open, do not turn your face away from the horror of this moment, but use your love to work to ensure that my grief will be an echo of the past."[34] He remembers Marvin Gaye and how he "used his artistic skill to inspire the world to raise the question not only 'What's going on' but 'Makes Me Want to Holler.'"[35] He speaks of Martin Luther King Jr.'s quest to fight for justice in the face of injustice. Finally, he concludes with the ministry of Jesus and how Jesus "spent his entire ministry being an advocate for those who had no advocate."[36]

In response to this conversation with his father, Moss's son left his father's arms, took paper and pen, and began to draw a picture of Trayvon Martin with his arms around Emmitt Till. Of his son's response, Moss says, "What theology, what imagination! When his heart was breaking, he reached into the imagination given to him by God and began to draw a new world. Maybe there is a great lesson for us, all of God's people, that we have all been called not to wallow in our pain but to pull out our pen and dip it in the ink of our souls and draw onto the canvas of injustice a picture that has not yet been drawn."[37] Moss adapts his personal conversation with his son into a moment of hope and inspiration for the congregation at large. Not only did he give them a window into their pain and grief; he invited them into the moment and method of hope that followed.

Rev. Dr. Renita J. Weems, "Scream" (Riverside Church, New York City)

On February 20, 2015, the Riverside Church of New York City held a service titled "Seven Last Words: Strange Fruit Speaks." This program took on the same format as the traditional Good Friday service centered on the seven last words from the cross. Instead of Jesus's final words, this program focused on the final words of people of color killed by state-sponsored violence. The presenters on that night were Rev. Traci Blackmon with "Mom, I Want to Go to College" (Amadou Diallo), Rosa A. Clemente with "Don't Shoot" (Michael Brown), Rev. Nyle Fort with "I Love You (Too)" (Sean Bell), Darnell L. Moore with "I Don't Want to Die" (Shantel Davis), Father Michael L. Pfleger with "I Want to Go Home" (Renisha McBride), Rev. Michael A. Walrond Jr. with "I Can't Breathe" (Eric Garner), and Dr. Renita Weems with "Scream" (Trayvon Martin). This format represented a powerful response in the Christian faith community to the ongoing movement for Black lives.

In her sermon on Trayvon, Dr. Renita J. Weems opens with a mission statement about the gathering itself: "Let's be clear. We do not gather tonight because we are afraid to die. We do not gather tonight because we cannot accept death. Let's be clear. We are not here tonight because we don't want to die. We accept death. What we do not and cannot accept is the senseless death of our children."[38] This striking introduction invokes that of a presiding officer at a funeral and serves as a somber reminder of the context of the specially-themed service. While the traditional seven last words services center on this dying moment of Jesus on the cross, this service was grounded in the dying moments but carried over into the aftermath of these seven tragic deaths. While Good Friday represents a moment of suffering before the celebratory climax of the resurrection, Trayvon and the others would have no physical resurrection in three days. This reality necessitates a different approach—one that pushes many preachers out of their comfort zone.

What does it mean to preach lament? When there is no celebratory close, just the lingering reality of loss, what are we as people of faith to do? And how do we approach the preaching moment? How do we preach the good news of Jesus Christ amid current tragedy? The gospel cannot be confined to personal salvation after death. In times of tragedy and injustice, the will to fight for righteousness is itself good news. That God would empower us with a prophetic voice to tear down structures of oppression is itself good news. The temptation for pastors is to encourage by pointing to the afterlife when things will get better, but with unjust deaths all around, such preaching amounts to a cruel jest to point to more death as the only path to peace and righteousness. This type of tragedy requires more than just giving hope for a brighter future. It requires abiding in the discomfort of the moment and spurring the listeners to action that will create that brighter future.

For Dr. Weems, this meant preaching from a place of personal identity and truth, in her case a uniquely female perspective. She stated, "I'm not trying to make this a gendered sermon, but it must become a gendered sermon." Indeed, a sermon preached by a Black woman will and should shine a light on issues of gender and race that another would not. While the concept was framed around Trayvon's last scream for help, the sermon preached through Dr. Weems's Black woman lens seemed to speak more from the perspective of Trayvon's mother, Sybrina Fulton. Of Trayvon's final scream, Weems says, "Sometimes crying and weeping and wailing are the only appropriate things that can be done, Trayvon. And so, as a seventeen-year-old young boy, his last words were not a sentence with a noun and a subject, a noun and a verb, were not a sentence with an infinitive or a preposition. His last words were a SCREAM! A boy screamed because he was a child, and children in trouble scream."[39] However, she makes a significant turn by giving voice to the screams of Trayvon's mother and other women saying, "Those of us who not only are 'sun kissed' but are also 'female kissed,' we understand the importance and the significance of tears or crying."[40] While the tragedy of Trayvon losing his life is front and center, it takes another Black woman to see through the perspective of a mother who lost her child.

Not only did Weems preach from a uniquely female perspective, but she also preached through the lens of an older Black woman. She identified herself, along with Father Michael Pfleger, as the oldest presenters on the platform. So, in addition to her unique perspective as a Black woman, she brought a significant generational perspective. In this way, her sermon embodied Gilbert's sagely preaching voice. Surprisingly, she offered an apology on behalf of her generation to those younger than her:

> We owe your generation an apology. We thought we had nailed things down for you. We thought we were passing on to you a better future, a more secure future. It's not that we thought that race had been conquered; we thought that at least we had given you a system and bequeathed to you a system where there was redress. We thought, in our youthfulness and in our rashness and in our naïveté, . . . with the student movement and with the anti-war and anti-Vietnam movement and . . . with women's rights, that we could pass on to you a better world.[41]

Like Solomon in Ecclesiastes, she remembers the days of her youth and laments the ultimate ineffectiveness of her actions. This is significant since Weems comes from a generation of activists who challenged the prevailing systems and made major advancements in civil rights, women's rights, and others. She represents the generation of Selma and Stonewall and is herself the fulfillment of the

Seneca Falls dream. Yet despite all those advancements, none of them could stop Trayvon, Mike Brown, Renisha McBride, or any of the others from losing their lives to a still broken system. This honest expression of disappointment and helplessness is a necessary part of calling the community of faith together to mourn and ultimately respond to the prevailing evil in this world.

Summary

Each of the selected sermons offers a unique perspective on a common event. Callahan and Ray offer the most pastoral of the responses. Using the same text, Luke 10, they challenge the listeners in their respective congregations to do more than point fingers of accusation at injustice in society, but rather to examine themselves and how we all have been perpetrators of injustice in our lives. They cover the prophetic base of identifying the injustice that was on the minds and hearts of the people, but to minister to their souls requires more than the identification of a societal ill—it requires the will to challenge the listener to self-examination. This call to reflection and repentance is a priestly task in which pastors must be versed.

Both Callahan and Ray show that prophetic sermons are not the only dangerous sermons, but the priestly call to personal accountability epitomizes Thomas's moral imagination and represents a tangible risk to the pastor. No one enjoys being called to personal responsibility. It is not comfortable to be confronted with one's own bias or fear or racism. But to move toward a more just society, preachers must do more than celebrate the righteous— they must challenge those who think they are righteous to confront their own faults. What LaRue characterizes as the domain of personal piety must be anchored in a call to love one another. The issues that led to Trayvon's death and Zimmerman's acquittal are not confined to the realm of social justice. They are inherently caused by a lack of personal and communal morality. To effect change, the preacher must address this in the hearts of the listening congregation.

Wesley, Moss, and Weems offer responses rooted in their identities and the intersection of their experiences as Black men (Wesley and Moss) and as a Black woman (Weems). Wesley and Moss speak from their position as not only Black men but also fathers of Black boys. From this, their perspective was primarily rooted in Trayvon's identity and the parallels between him and their own sons. For Weems, the point of intersection was less with Trayvon and more with Sybrina Fulton, his mother. While Trayvon's final scream as recorded on the 911 call was the precipitating muse for her title and theme, the imagery of Fulton's screams of grief upon losing her child dominated the content of Weems's sermon. These sermons rooted in Black man and Black woman identities clearly illustrate LaRue's corporate concerns domain of experience. As LaRue states, "Certain issues and interests in Black life arise out of its unique history and cultural experiences in this country."[42] In times of communal trauma, the shared experiences of Blackness, womanhood, or any other defining domains of culture and experience are tools to draw from for collective healing.

Reflection Questions before You Preach

1. Should I preach this now, or should I sit with it for a week or more?

2. Am I being emotionally honest?

3. What is my aim? To comfort the afflicted or afflict the comfortable?

4. Am I preaching to my actual audience, or am I speaking truth to a power that will never hear this sermon?

5. Will this sermon sufficiently address specific cultural and communal needs?

Notes
1. "Herstory," July 5, 2019, https://blacklivesmatter.com/about/herstory/.
2. Ibid.
3. Ibid.
4. "Herstory," September 21, 2022, https://blacklivesmatter.com/herstory//
5. Marvin A. McMickle, *The Making of a Preacher: Five Essentials for Today's Ministers* (Valley Forge, PA: Judson Press, 2018).
6. Sybrina Fulton and Tracy Martin, *Rest in Power: A Parents' Story of Love, Injustice, and the Birth of a Movement* (New York: Spiegel & Grau, 2017).
7. Ibid., 187.
8. @SybrinaFulton (Sybrina Fulton), "Lord during my darkest hour I lean on you. You are all that I have. At the end of the day, GOD is still in control. Thank you all for your prayers and support. I will love you forever Trayvon!!! In the name of Jesus!!!", Twitter, July 13, 2013, https://twitter.com/SybrinaFulton/status/356248501421735936.
9. @BTraymartin9 (Tracy Martin), "Even though I am broken hearted my faith is unshattered I WILL ALWAYS LOVE MY BABY TRAY," Twitter, July 13, 2013, https://twitter.com/BTraymartin9/status/356238887158431747.
10. Fulton and Martin.
11. Lizette Alvarez and Cara Buckley, "Zimmerman Is Acquitted in Trayvon Martin Killing," *New York Times*, July 13, 2013, https://www.nytimes.com/2013/07/14/us/george-zimmerman-verdict-trayvon-martin.html.
12. Ibid.
13. Leslie Callahan, "Neighborhood Watch," St. Paul's Baptist Church, Philadelphia, July 14, 2013; also preached at Samuel Dewitt Proctor Institute for Child Advocacy, Clinton, TN, July 19, 2013, https://www.youtube.com/watch?v=-pjxpnVQvYg.
14. Ibid.
15. Richard Wright, "The Ethics of Living Jim Crow" (1937), https://www.scarsdaleschools.k12.ny.us/cms/lib/NY01001205/Centricity/Domain/908/AT%20Ethics%20of%20Jim%20Crow.pdf.
16. Callahan.
17. Ibid.
18. Ibid.
19. Ibid.
20. The Emerging Church (formerly Community Christian Church), Springfield, MO, www.spfccc.org.
21. Roger L. Ray, "Trayvon Is Dead and None of Us Are 'Not Guilty,'" The Emerging Church (formerly Community Christian Church), Springfield, MO, July 14, 2013, https://youtu.be/4BqDYwaMygA.
22. Ibid.

23. Peter Finley Dunne, *Observations by Mr. Dooley* (New York: Harper and Brothers, 1906).

24. Elizabeth Dias, "The Best Sermon About Trayvon That You Will Hear," *Time*, July 18, 2013, http://swampland.time.com/2013/07/18/the-best-sermon-about-trayvon-that-you-will-hear/.

25. Howard-John Wesley, "When the Verdict Hurts," Alfred Street Baptist Church, Alexandria, Virginia, July 14, 2013, https://www.youtube.com/watch?v=hqhOe85_vA8.

26. Ibid.

27. Cleophas J. LaRue, *The Heart of Black Preaching* (Louisville, KY: Westminster John Knox, 2000).

28. Wesley.

29. Ibid.

30. Otis Moss III, "A Word for Trayvon," Trinity United Church of Christ, Chicago, July 14, 2013, https://www.youtube.com/watch?v=X7FhMwHi-lE.

31. Ibid.

32. Ibid.

33. Ibid.

34. Ibid.

35. Ibid.

36. Ibid.

37. Ibid.

38. Renita J. Weems, "Scream," Riverside Church, New York City, February 20, 2015, https://www.youtube.com/watch?v=2gPB-w2XP5Y.

39. Ibid.

40. Ibid.

41. Ibid.

42. LaRue, 23.

CHAPTER 5

The Four Tasks of Current Event Preaching

Common Approaches and Self-Evaluation

After examining a cross section of sermons preached in the wake of the Trayvon Martin shooting and the not guilty verdict in the trial of George Zimmerman, we turn our attention to some of the common approaches used in those preaching moments. From the five sermons that we examined in the previous chapter, we can identify four common categories of thematic response that I call the four tasks of current event preaching. They are honesty and vulnerability, metaphoric parallelism, prophetic remembrance toward hope, and finally, a call to action. These four tasks represent a homiletic map to guide the construction of sermons that respond to notable events, whether they are local incidents or national headlines.

The goal of using this framework is to apply all four tasks in the preaching moment, safeguarding against incomplete or ineffective sermonic responses.

Task 1: Honesty and Vulnerability

When responding to emotionally draining or traumatic events, it is important to be honest and to show the ability to be vulnerable. Most of the selected sermons contained some type of disclaimer, such as a statement like "I'm still processing this" or "I don't really understand this." In circumstances like these, the congregation does not need an expert to explain—rather, they need a partner in lament. Only through empathy can a preacher gain permission to give hope. The honest display of vulnerability invites the congregation to walk hand in hand through the tension of the moment toward the hope found in God.

In the sermon "Neighborhood Watch," Dr. Callahan provides a window into her own process and invites the listeners into collective reflection. She states, "I think many of us have the same thing on our minds, and I have been trying over the last couple of days, actually the last year and a half, to try to make sense of what is going on, of what happened to Trayvon Martin and then more recently the verdict in Florida, and so I am going to do a bit of reflecting on that tonight."[1] Importantly, she offers a strong disclaimer: "I don't hope to answer the question[s]; they still are going around in my mind, but I'm not going to avoid them."[2] The task of the preacher is not to answer all the questions, but rather to join the congregation in posing the questions before the all-knowing God at peace with the mystery of our own finite minds. If we had to understand everything that we preach about, we would never preach about some things. On the contrary, the task of the preacher is not to understand or explain but to point to God.

To willfully display a lack of understanding sounds counterproductive, but this type of honesty works to reassure often skeptical listeners and invite them into the process of spiritual reflection. Renita Weems displays considerable honesty saying, "Gatherings like these represent our collective attempt as people of faith to make sense of the senselessness of it all. Senseless. And here we are activists and preachers, hell raisers, young and old pretending to be able to make sense of it, pretending that it can be explained and named and traced and exegeted and preached about."[3] Likewise, Otis Moss III says, "My mind is not able to conceive the weight of grief carried upon the shoulders of the Martin family."[4] No one is served by a preacher pretending to understand what is not understandable. The power is in asking the questions, even when an answer is not yet present. Weems offers a powerful litany on this subject:

> I don't know how to make sense of the unanswered cries for help of a boy in Sanford, Florida.
> I don't know how to make sense of Michael Brown's body lying facedown in blood for four hours in the middle of the street.
> I don't know how to make sense of a young girl being shot in the face through a screen door for stumbling on a stranger's doorstep and asking for help.
> How do we make sense of scenes like these repeatedly existing in the twenty-first century?[5]

Howard-John Wesley was perhaps the most emotional of the selected preachers, appearing visibly distraught at times and displaying honesty and vulnerability from the start of his sermon. He began the message by stating, "I have to be honest this morning, that I find it difficult to stand here as Reverend Doctor, because as Reverend Doctor, you have the expectation that I am super spiritual and somehow or another shielded from the realities of the struggles of life that we all experience. I want to ask you to give me a little bit of time to take off the Reverend, Doctor, Pastor, and just put on the Howard-John for a moment."[6] This purposeful display of duality serves two purposes: it gives an honest disclaimer to the mental, spiritual, and emotional state that the sermon was delivered in, and it makes the pastor and the message accessible to those in the congregation who were also having difficulty in the wake of the verdict.

Wesley openly struggled with the conflicting emotions of hurt, confusion, disappointment, and anger. He was candid as he attempted to give a balanced word to the congregation at Alfred

Street Baptist Church. "As I stand here like most of you, I come with a mixed bag of emotions. In one way I'm hurt, I hurt with Trayvon Martin's mother and father, I hurt."[7] Beyond being hurt, and even more significant, he indicated that he was confused both legally and theologically. This state of confusion further illustrated his initial disclaimer and why it was necessary for him to take off his "Reverend Doctor" and put on his "Howard-John." The attempt to fill the role of reverend, doctor, scholar, pastor, sage, prophet, counselor, or any other number of roles a preacher is called to operate in can be both daunting and detrimental to the health of the preacher. It is also often ineffective. Congregations that are hurting in the moment do not need someone doing theology from above, offering canned exegesis and convenient explanations for the ills of this broken world. They need a human being who incarnates their struggle and offers empathetic guidance as they walk together—the kind of incarnational empathy modeled by Jesus of Nazareth.

Honesty and vulnerability are what McMickle calls "confessing your character"[8] and what Thomas frames as "empathy as catalyst or bridge"[9] in the second quality of moral imagination. It also exemplifies Gilbert's priestly voice as one of humility and self-reflection. The display of honesty and vulnerability guards against the risk of the preacher detailing the sins of the listener or society without "tears in their own eyes."[10] To be truly effective, a sermon must connect on an emotional level with the listening audience. This requires a level of empathy that can be expressed only through vulnerability and the will to express it openly and honestly.

Task 2: Metaphoric Parallelism

Another common approach in the selected sermons is metaphoric parallelism. Metaphoric parallelism is the analogous linking of narratives from the biblical text or other historic contexts to a similar event or situation in the preacher's current context. This approach is common in most narrative expository sermons as parallels are drawn between the biblical characters and contemporary contexts, but it is especially relevant when viewing contemporary events through the lens of the biblical narrative.

In addition to the parable of the Good Samaritan, Dr. Callahan quotes Jeremiah 31:15, which also anchors Moss's address: "Thus says the Lord: A voice is heard in Ramah, lamentation and bitter weeping. Rachel is weeping for her children; she refuses to be comforted for her children, because they are no more." The relevance of this text is striking when considering the plight of Sybrina Fulton (mother of Trayvon Martin), Lesley McSpadden (mother of Mike Brown), and countless other mothers weeping for their children lost to state-sponsored violence. Both Callahan and Moss use Rachel's plight in the text as a parallel to Trayvon's family's plight, as well as those who mourn in solidarity with them. By telling the story of Rachel, they simultaneously tell the story of Sybrina Fulton and others. While Callahan and Moss bring Rachel's cries to remembrance, Weems moves beyond Rachel and gives voice to Hagar and Ishmael. "As God said to Hagar, 'I know you're crying, but I have heard the cries of the little boy, and because of the little boy, I will save the people of Ishmael.' Tonight, Hagar may be crying, Rachel may be crying, but God says, 'I have heard the cries of the little boy.' Thanks be to God, God heard Trayvon's cry."[11] In this parallel, Ishmael's cries become the cries of Trayvon, and God heard Trayvon's cry just as God heard Ishmael's.

Wesley finds his parallel in the passion of Jesus Christ. As he makes his turn to Scripture, he beckons the congregation to "come on out of 2013 and journey back to antiquity in Jerusalem with me and allow me to show you another travesty of justice. A brother is on trial, some of y'all don't know him, his name is Jesus. And he's brought up on some charges that have no validity."[12] The notion of an unjust Zimmerman verdict is juxtaposed with the unjust verdict handed down by Pontius Pilate upon Jesus Christ. Wesley's title "When the Verdict Hurts" now takes on a completely different meaning. While Wesley and the members of Alfred Street that day bore the mental and emotional toll of the Zimmerman verdict the night before, in the case of Jesus, the verdict hurt literally and physically in the form of a cat o' nine tails and nails holding him to the cross. Preachers in the Black Baptist tradition are notorious (for better or worse) for finding creative ways to "get to the cross" in their sermonic close, but in Wesley's case, it was both relevant and appropriate. Jesus viscerally bores the weight of his verdict the way others figuratively bore the weight of the Zimmerman verdict.

In addition to Jesus himself, Wesley also turns to Simon of Cyrene:

> Simon, verse 21 says, is compelled to carry the cross . . . he did not do it of his own volition. That word *compelled* is a euphemistic way of saying that the same Roman government who found Jesus guilty even though he was innocent are now the soldiers who force Simon to carry the weight of the cross that is the result of an unjust verdict. Here is a brother who now has to bear a weight that is the result of an unjust verdict. He has no choice in the matter, he cannot escape it, the reality is he's got to learn to carry that weight. Good morning, Simon, because that's what you have to learn to do today, to carry the weight that comes as the result of an unjust verdict. And we're compelled to do it, not because we want to but because it's done.[13]

The turn of phrase "Good morning, Simon" is Wesley's way of drawing the congregation into the narrative. As Simon bore the weight of Jesus's cross, so did they have a cross to bear in the wake of an unjust verdict.

Wesley then turns from his picture of Simon to the effect on his children. He links Simon's son Rufus in Mark 15 to the Rufus mentioned in Romans 16: "The young boy who watches his father carry the weight is the young boy who winds up in Rome itself proclaiming the good news of Jesus Christ. The same young boy who watched his daddy bear that weight is the young man that grew up and stood in the middle of the same city and declared Jesus is Lord!"[14] After showing the impact of that verdict on Simon's sons, Wesley turns the attention to his own children and the children of the listening audience. "The way his father carried the weight allowed that young man to be productive in the center of a system that was biased against him. We have to carry this weight correctly because we've got some Rufus[es] and Alexanders who are watching how we respond to this."[15] The metaphoric parallel was used as both a reminder of history and a call to present action.

For Otis Moss III, after detailing the conversation in which his son asked, "Daddy, am I next?" and after speaking of young Moss's picture of Trayvon embracing Emmitt Till, Dr. Moss builds a metaphoric litany around the question, What shall we draw?

> Maybe our art teacher is Amos, and Amos gives us instruction to draw and say, "Let justice roll down like waters and righteousness as a mighty stream."
>
> Maybe we should draw like Isaiah. "Seek justice, encourage the oppressed, defend the fatherless, and plead the case of the widow."
>
> Maybe we should draw like Jesus. "For the spirit of the Lord is upon us to preach the good news to the poor, to proclaim freedom to the prisoner, recovery of the sight to the blind, and set the oppressed free."
>
> Maybe we should draw like Micah and "do justice, love kindness, walk humbly with our God."
>
> Maybe we should draw as Dr. King says knowing that "the arc of the universe is long, but it bends toward justice."

Maybe we should draw as [James] Russell Lowell says, "Truth forever on the scaffold, wrong forever on the throne, yet that scaffold sways the future, and, behind the dim unknown, stands God within the shadow, keeping watch above his own."

Or maybe in the words of James Weldon Johnson we need to draw a new picture. "God of our weary years, God of our silent tears, thou who has brought us thus far on the way, thou who has by thy might led us into the light, keep us forever on the path, we pray."[16]

The metaphor of drawing is the dominant thread of Moss's message. Not only does it serve as a link between the profound act of artistic response by his son and the biblical text, but Moss extends the metaphor to more contemporary examples. In his use of the term, to "draw" means to respond, to act, to take the injustice of the moment and rework it for a just future. His son's artistic creation became an act of resistance and hope. From the shocking words "am I next" came an expression of beauty. Black preachers, poets, and artists of various stripes have a history of taking trauma and somehow turning it into something beautiful. This does not trivialize the impact of the traumatic event, but it does empower our creative response and awaken the resiliency that generations of tragedy have taught us.

Metaphoric parallelism serves two primary purposes. First, it provides a tangible connection with the biblical text, thereby making the ancient wisdom current and accessible. This echoes Thomas's third quality of moral imagination, which is "find wisdom in ancient texts, sources of ancient wisdom and truth, the wisdom of the ages."[17] Metaphoric parallelism also fulfills the fourth quality of Thomas's moral imagination, which is "the language of poetry and art that lifts and elevates the human spirit by touching the emotive chords of wonder, mystery, and hope."[18] Metaphor itself is a central element of poetry, and its use in conjunction with other poetic elements such as alliteration and the construction of repetitive litanies like Moss's "Maybe we should draw . . ." amplifies the emotive connection with the listener.

LaRue points to creative language uses as one of the central characteristics of Black preaching. He says, "The traditional Black church expects and appreciates rhetorical flair and highly poetic language in the preaching of the gospel . . . Unlike many European and mainline American denominations, where architecture and classical music inspire a sense of the holy, Blacks seek to accomplish this act through the display of well-crafted rhetoric."[19] Likewise, Croft points to four stylistic traits of Black preaching: "rhythm and musical sound, call and response, poetic language and imagery and storytelling."[20] Poetic language, in general, is a common distinctive in Black preaching, while metaphoric parallelism in particular is effective in reconciling the wisdom of the text with the events of everyday life.

Task 3: Prophetic Remembrance Toward Hope

The point of metaphoric parallelism is to convey the message that we've been here before—a point that was driven home in explicit terms by several of the preachers. Conveying this message of remembrance is a prophetic act. In Hebrew Scripture, the exodus is regularly called to the Israelites' memory as a reminder of God's faithfulness to deliver in the past and as a source of hope for the present and future. African American churches facing the murder of unarmed Black youth and a largely unsympathetic justice system turn to the biblical text to draw the inspiration to persevere. Metaphoric parallelism as prophetic remembrance fits John McClure's definition of prophetic preaching as "an imaginative reappropriation of traditional narratives and symbols for the purpose of critiquing a dangerous and unjust present situation and providing an alternative vision of God's future."[21] However, one key difference exists in this context: the purpose of reappropriating the traditional narratives is not simply to critique an unjust present situation. Rather, the purpose is to provide hope to the victims of the unjust present situation by pointing to biblical narratives or more recent examples of injustice and importantly to those who survived and overcame them.

Like the ancient Israelites, Black churches can look to the exodus from Egyptian slavery, or we can look to the gospel narrative of Jesus overcoming death and the grave. We can also call to remembrance our own most recent history. From chattel slavery to emancipation, from Jim Crow to integration, remembering the past gives hope for the future, if by nothing else, showing that we can survive. Remembrance of the past is what gives evidence for hope in the future. James Evans says, "A hope that does not come to terms with history can become unbridled optimism and idealism, or the cover for unchecked expansionism. History anchors hope. Because history and hope always belong to a specific community, they can mean different things to different people."[22] The task of the preacher is to define the terms of future hope based on remembrance of a shared history.

The selected sermons commonly begin with social commentary and critique of an unjust system but then transition to prophetic remembrance and hope. When Howard-John Wesley makes the turn toward Scripture around the 10:30 mark of his twenty-eight-minute sermon, he opens this portion of the sermon with the turning phrase "This is not the first time we've had to learn to live with a verdict that hurts."[23] This is a clear example of a prophetic call to remembrance. He then uses the gospel message of Jesus's crucifixion and resurrection as hope for the congregation. He does the same in his metaphoric portrayal of Simon of Cyrene with another important parallel—Simon's African identity. Wesley draws attention to this African identity and the Passover, which was his reason for being in Jerusalem.

Passover, in Wesley's words, is "the season where the Jews gathered together and looked back at what God did in Egypt and reminded themselves of the God that brought them this far."[24] Since Simon is from Cyrene, which is in Africa, Wesley paints him as "a brother who is in Passover mindset . . . reflecting over where the Lord has brought his people."[25] By calling attention to Simon, the African celebrating Passover, Wesley is calling his congregation filled with people of African descent to do the same. "Here is an African who is in Passover mindset, here is a brother that's come out of Africa and is remembering where the Lord has brought him from, and he finds the strength to carry the weight of an unjust verdict because he's an African who's come so far that he remembers where the Lord has brought him from."[26] To remember the past is to find the courage to face present difficulties. Wesley continues, "That is where we find the strength to bear this weight, because if anybody ought to remember what the Lord has done, it ought to be those who have some genes in Africa. Those who know the Lord has brought us up out of Africa, carried us through slavery, and brought us to where we are right now."[27] He then offers a litany that perfectly illustrates prophetic remembrance as a catalyst for hope.

> We have dealt with this before!
> He carried us through Emmitt Till.
> He carried us through the Sixteenth Street Baptist Church in Birmingham, Alabama.
> He carried us through James Bird and Yusef Hawkins.
> He carried us through Rodney King.
> And God will carry us through this![28]

Perhaps the greatest summary of prophetic remembrance came from this line delivered by Wesley: "We find our strength to bear this, knowing that our forefathers and foremothers have walked this road before."[29] To know that the road has been walked before supplies the strength to keep walking.

The rich tradition of Black music, hymns, and poetry is a valuable conduit to prophetic remembrance. Both Moss and Wesley quote James Weldon Johnson's "Lift Every Voice and Sing," with Wesley drawing from the second verse.

> We have come over a way that with tears has been watered,
>> and we have come treading our path through the blood of the slaughtered.[30]

"... and the God that carried us through all of that is the God that gives us strength to carry this weight."[31] The hymns of the church have long been a source of hope and strength, and the hymnbook is one of the sacred texts of the church. The Black preaching tradition often calls upon the lyrics of hymns during the celebratory close. This reaching back into the verses of hymns is not just to remember the past but to draw hope and strength for the future and for the present. The task of giving hope is a matter of survival. To give hope at the close of the preached word on Sunday morning is preparation for the week that is ahead. It is the equipping of the saints to stay focused on the goodness of God when the news cycle is filled with death and destruction. It is the hope of the gospel that pushes us to press forward when pessimism tells us to give up. Prophetic remembrance is drawing from a well of hope that will propel us into the future.

Note, in the case of Wesley's "When the Verdict Hurts" and other effective sermons, the prophetic call to remembrance happens in the conclusion of the message, after there has been a period of reflection and lament. While hope should be the goal of any sermon, it cannot be delivered at the expense of solemn reflection. There is no shortcut to hope. It must be built through the process of reflection, lament, and remembrance. Jumping to hope without acknowledging and processing the traumatic event of the moment is a mistake. To jump to hope without reflection is dismissive of the emotional and spiritual toll that traumatic events play in people's lives. A hasty move toward hope amounts to a psychologist telling a client to "just get over it," or a eulogist telling a grieving family, "Don't cry; you should be rejoicing." Not only is this tactic harsh and crude, but it also lacks the empathy necessary to effectively minister.

Wesley earned the spiritual capital necessary to give hope by first honestly and openly wrestling with the very real feelings of hurt, confusion, disappointment, and anger that he shared with the congregation. The task of the pastor/preacher in moments of collective grief or trauma is not to arbitrarily give hope but to walk with the congregation through each stage with empathy, compassion, and understanding. In the words attributed to Theodore Roosevelt, "No one cares how much you know until they know how much you care." The task of giving lasting hope must follow prophetic remembrance and pastoral empathy.

Task 4: Call to Action

There is surely hope in the resurrection of Jesus Christ and the assuredness of a future in heaven when this broken world has passed away. But as Croft illustrates in his examination of nineteenth-century preaching, an eschatological hope for the future does not replace the need for hope in this world. Hope for now requires action right now, in this current world. Martin Luther King Jr. often spoke of the "fierce urgency of now" and in doing so became what Noel Erskine called "the classic representation of those during slavery who combined eschatological hope for future blessedness with moral witness and political action in the present."[32] Effective preaching must address current realities and then go beyond words to inspire a response in the listener. This is what Howard Thurman means when he says, "Mere preaching is not enough. What are words, however sacred and powerful, in the presence of the grim facts of the daily struggle to survive?"[33] The call to action is instruction on what to do with the hope that the sermon has instilled. This is what Moss is doing when he calls on the people to pick up their metaphoric pens and draw a new reality and what Wesley did at the close of his message.

Wesley, in classic celebratory fashion, points to the hope of the resurrection, but while this celebration represents the climax of his preaching moment, he does not end there. He says:

> What we have the [benefit] of knowing that Simon didn't was that, yes, that Jesus was crucified but . . . early on Sunday morning he would rise from the dead! That message of the resurrection of Jesus is not just a button to push at the end of a sermon to make folks stand up and shout. It is a hope that lies within us that declares that no matter how bad it gets, we serve a God who if you give him some time and put your faith in him and trust in him, he is able to turn situations around, he is able to resurrect dead things, he is able! The message of the resurrected Jesus is this, that the verdict, though unjust, is not the end of the story.[34]

This is the classic close on the hope of the empty tomb, "but early on Sunday morning"—five words that have excited Black churches for generations. What is more significant is what happens after "but early." In Wesley's sermon, after he points to the hope of the resurrection, he issues a simple one-line call to action. In conclusion, he says,

I don't know how, when, where God does it and will resurrect it, but my faith says that God makes things right, my faith says that God knows how to handle situations like this, my faith says that one day I'll see the justice that I demand. It may not be in this life, but I'm so glad this ain't the only life I'm living for. For when this old life is over, I've got another home not made with human hands where there's nothing but glory and justice all day long! And God will wipe every tear from our eyes. And God will hold the heart of Trayvon Martin's parents. And God will comfort us through this situation. We've got to handle it correctly.[35]

It is that last line, the final six words of the twenty-eight-minute sermon, that represents the call to action. After every stage, after the honesty, after the lament, after the prophetic remembrance, after the hope of the resurrection, the listener is left with questions like What do I do with this? What are the next steps? How do we emerge from this equipped to move on? For Wesley, this is summarized in the words "We've got to handle it correctly."[36]

Dr. Callahan's message gives considerable attention on how to handle the verdict and aftermath correctly, and she found guidance in the words of someone she described as a "conspiracy theorist" on social media. According to Callahan, this conspiracy theorist surmised:

The reason why the verdict came back on Saturday night was because, as he put it, "Negroes will be in church tomorrow hearing about forgiveness and learning to be quiet." He surmised that what it would mean for us to be in church yesterday morning is that we would be calmed down and our anger would be defused and our sense of outrage at the injustice would be defused, and we'd go home feeling good about having gotten our praise on, on Sunday morning, and we would not do a blessed thing![37]

This take challenged Callahan, and it made her realize that "the world is looking at us and listening to us." Returning to her neighborhood motif, she says:

> Our neighborhood is watching to see whether we who are pious, whether those of us who are the professionally religious will walk by the broken and the broke, whether those of us who pay our tithes and fast and pray during Lent will walk by the people who are hurting in our community. The people in our neighborhood are watching us, they're listening to see what we will say.[38]

The question of how we handle this correctly is not just one for the preacher or pastor preparing the message to consider, but one that everyone in the listening audience should consider as they leave the sanctuary and return to their daily lives.

Returning attention to the Good Samaritan text, Callahan quotes Martin Luther King Jr., saying:

> On the one hand we are called to play the good Samaritan on life's roadside. But that will be only an initial act. One day we must come to see that the whole Jericho Road must be transformed so that men and women will not be constantly beaten and robbed as they make their journey on life's highway. True compassion is more than flinging a coin to a beggar. It is not haphazard and superficial; it comes to see that an edifice which produces beggars needs restructuring.[39]

It is not enough to call out societal injustice, nor is it sufficient to give empty hope that "everything's gonna be all right." After the church has cried, shouted, sat in silence, or whatever other emotive responses have been invoked, the listening congregation must leave with a clarion call to action and an answer to the question, How do we handle this correctly?

Part of the call to action is by necessity taking sides. Neutrality is the enemy of action. Roger L. Ray says:

> Don't presume that I'm neutral here. Neutrality is the job of almost every other preacher you're ever going to meet. I'm here to tell you that I believe that the good Samaritan made a good choice, and that George Zimmerman made a bad choice. I want you to make the right choice. And until it's safe to walk while being Black in America, all of us need to keep exposing the hypocrisy of the nation that we live in and have helped to create.[40]

Ray is definitive about the choices that people make, although he gives a balanced and nuanced account of Zimmerman's actions. Ultimately, Ray is clear that Zimmerman made a bad choice, and the congregants of the Emerging Church that day were challenged to consider their own choices. Ray says, "Decide who you want to be. Do you want revenge? Or do you want to become the kind of person that has the nobility of spirit to be forgiving? Do you want to feel safe and empowered and aggressive? Or do you want to choose to be vulnerable enough to love your enemy, and to show kindness even to someone who doesn't deserve it?"[41]

In summarizing the parable of the Good Samaritan, Ray says, "Jesus told the story of a man who chose to be bigger than his fear, bigger than his anger, bigger than his sense of having been victimized or his need for safety or revenge."[42] Drawing from the text, he challenged the congregation to overcome their deeply embedded personal faults and biases to make decisions in line with the teachings of Jesus. This call to action is the task of every preacher.

Since preaching includes the task of honesty and vulnerability, I now will evaluate and reflect on two sermons that I preached after the Trayvon Martin verdict.

Rev. Clarence E. Wright, "When God Talks Back" (Love Zion Baptist Church, Philadelphia)

Self-Evaluation

On Sunday, July 14, 2013, I was three months removed from my installation as the second pastor of the Love Zion Baptist Church in Philadelphia and roughly ten months beyond taking over weekly preaching duties after the death of our organizing pastor. Although I had been preaching for seventeen years at the time, I had not yet begun seminary studies, and I was very new to the role of senior pastor. The task of preaching the morning after the verdict represented one of my early preaching challenges as pastor. Unlike Dr. Wesley and others, I did not come out of the preaching series that I was in. At the time, I was on part two of a series entitled "Overflow," in which I was preaching through the book of 2 Chronicles. My next sermon was already scheduled to come from 2 Chronicles 7:14. I felt God's promise in the text to heal the land was appropriate considering the lingering effects of the verdict, so I elected to stick with it and preached from the topic "When God Talks Back." While I technically covered the four tasks of current event preaching, the content nevertheless left much room for improvement.

I spoke extensively about the verdict in the introduction but kept most of the exegetical work that I had already prepared for the rest of the sermon. Early on I laid my cards on the table, expressing my feelings about the verdict:

> I believe George Zimmerman to be at least guilty of manslaughter and perhaps second-degree murder. However, I refuse to contribute to the vitriol on this morning after. I refuse to pick up my verbal pitchfork and join the lynch mob. No matter what an easy preach it may be, I refuse to fan the flames of furor. We are already angry; the last thing you need is for your pastor to make you angrier.

These words reflect my state of mind when the verdict was issued late the Saturday night before. My mind immediately went back to 1992, when South Central Los Angeles was burned and looted in the wake of the Rodney King verdict. Although the Martin family had handled themselves with the utmost dignity during the entire trial, there was nevertheless a palpable fear that this verdict would spark something ugly. Social media had already exploded with reaction, and there was uncertainty over what would be next. Although I was angry, I saw my role as a peacemaker, calling the people to prayer and humble submission to the will of God. I did what I thought at the time a good pastor should do. Looking back, however, my approach feels passive-aggressive at best and dismissive at worst. While I succeeded in being honest about my own feelings of anger, my tone lacked the vulnerability required to show empathy. I instead chose a position of pietism, assuming the worst of the congregation's motives and warning them not to give in to those base instincts.

Part of the introduction was an intentionally ironic play on words, where I talked about all the things that I was not going to talk about.

> I will not be giving fiery commentary on the injustice of this nation's judicial system. I will not lament about the sad reality of racial profiling and the systematic degradation of

people of color in America. I will not comment on how as a Black man in Philadelphia I am regularly pulled over for seemingly no reason. I will not be making any comparisons between Michael Vick and George Zimmerman or between dogs and Black boys. I will not commentate on the criminal injustice system. I am not wearing a hoodie today, although I thought about it. I will not preach a sermon about injustice, because talking about injustice will not make it go away.

The irony of talking about things I said I was not going to talk about was a mildly humorous play on words and a harmless poetic device. What is more concerning is the dismissive statement that "talking about injustice will not make it go away." My perspective has dramatically changed on this. I now see "talking about injustice" as not only an effective way to combat injustice but also a key function of preaching the gospel.

What is the gospel if not good news to the poor and liberty to the captives? My dismissive posture continued as I detailed my lack of shock at the verdict: "Am I upset? Yes . . . Am I shocked? No. Incensed? Yes . . . Shocked? No. Outraged? Yes . . . Shocked? No. I've been prepared for this verdict since the initial arrest was made. In fact, to me the biggest injustice was that it took so long for them to arrest him in the first place. Now the travesty on top of a tragedy that in my mind was always a probability has happened." Again, using repetitive litany and thematic juxtaposition, I made use of a poetic device but in the process compromised my honesty in the moment. I stand by my lack of shock, as I was genuinely not surprised at the verdict, but listening to my own words years later, it seems I was trying to curtail my emotions. Since I did not think it pastoral to be fully angry, I shrouded my anger in a cloak of "it is what it is"—a shoulder shrug of "there's nothing we can do but move on and humbly accept the will of God"—as if injustice is God's will.

Truthfully, I was every bit as angry and confused as Dr. Wesley was when he opened "When the Verdict Hurts," but fear and inexperience caused me to qualify and disguise what were genuine emotions, emotions that members of my congregation most certainly shared. While Wesley felt comfortable putting down the "Reverend Doctor" in favor of the "Howard-John," I clung tight to "Pastor Wright," a title that had been bestowed on me only months before. I was filling the role that I thought I was supposed to fill. In retrospect, my words were cautious and safe: "With the verdict that was handed down on Saturday night, how do I respond to this on Sunday morning? I could echo the common refrain, 'No justice, no peace.' I could advocate launching protests and revolutions, I could respond as an activist, but instead, I'll respond as a pastor, and as a pastor, all I can do is point you to the Word." Now I understand that pastor and activist are not in binary opposition to each other and pointing to the Word is only one small function of pastoral and prophetic leadership. Beyond pointing to the Word, the Word must be presented in a way that both comforts and calls to action.

From the text, I presented three main points about God's response to Solomon's prayer at the temple's completion: God responds with a warning, God responds with instruction, and God responds by hearing our prayer. I attempted to show that a cursed land does not necessarily mean a cursed people, with an emphasis on God's power to heal the cursed land if God's people would follow God's instructions, specifically, to humble themselves, pray, seek God's face, and turn from their wicked ways. Murder, racism, and all injustice were presented as symptoms of a cursed land in need of healing from God. All of this is in keeping with the task of metaphoric parallelism. The curse of drought and locusts in ancient Judah metaphorically became the curses of racism and injustice in twenty-first-century America, with God's promise of healing and forgiveness representing prophetic remembrance toward hope.

The power of prayer to "heal the land" was the overarching message of the sermon, with an unapologetic emphasis on the power of prayer alone:

> if you think that prayer is not enough, if you think I'm getting too spiritual, and that this isn't the time to pray but to fight, then you obviously don't know what prayer can do! If you think that, you don't really believe in prayer, because fighting has limitations, but there's nothing that prayer can't do! Prayer can heal the sick, prayer can raise the dead, prayer can change the minds of judges and juries, prayer can heal our communities, prayer can restore peace, prayer can lead to reconciliation! Keep protesting, but before you protest, pray; keep marching, but before you march, pray; keep speaking out against injustice, but while you're speaking, pray. And I believe that if you pray, not only will God hear your prayer, but God will respond to your prayer.

If I were preaching this sermon today, I would still emphasize the power of prayer, but I would put more emphasis on calling the people to action. Prayer is always needed, but through prayer, God also prepares us to fight. My call to action in this sermon was a call to prayer and fasting, which are important spiritual disciplines in which every Christian should be versed. However, a more pressing question is what to do when the prayer is over. When we say Amen and get off our knees, how do we work, through the aid of the Holy Spirit, to create a godlier world?

Regrettably, I feel I may be guilty of exactly what the "conspiracy theorist" predicted in Dr. Callahan's sermon. The thought of those "Negroes hearing about forgiveness and learning to be quiet" was piercing as I listened to my sermon from 2013.[43] The description of this social media conspiracist was eerily accurate, as my goal was to calm and defuse the anger and outrage of the people. Instead of comforting the people, giving them hope, and calling them to action, I chose to chastise them in an effort to police their emotions to prevent rioting or other violent response. The notion of humbling oneself and letting God handle it was a common refrain:

> Part of humbling yourself means admitting that you are not in control, there are some battles that only God can fight, there are some victories that only God can win. Part of humbling yourself means not trying to take justice in your own hands.
>
> The law doesn't always produce justice, but seeking justice independent of the law rarely works, especially when it involves violence.
>
> You've got to humble yourself and know that some things are out of your control.

Beyond being an oversimplification, this is also the language of gradualism and respectability, words that fortunately do not describe my ideology today. I've since learned that in the wake of national tragedies, particularly ones that directly affect the Black community, a better response is one of empathy, encouragement, and collective action, not a chastising, angry response.

Reflection

My preaching has undoubtedly grown since this example from the early months of my pastorate. I have made personal advancements in both theology and ideology. Still, there is always room for improvement. This exercise of self-evaluation and comparative analysis was eye-opening, and reflection on this sermon preached early in my pastorate would prove tremendously valuable, particularly in the turbulent days of 2020, as the next chapter will show. I hope you can benefit from my self-evaluation of a decade-old sermon, but I am certain you as a preacher would benefit even more from doing the same with your own past sermons. The temptation is often to look toward what's next, but much can be learned from looking back and being honest about what has changed and what can be improved.

After the initial research contained in this book, I began to intentionally apply the four tasks of current event preaching when major "Sunday after" moments arrived, and I became especially conscious of the need to be more honest and vulnerable. Beyond homiletic craft, I found a renewed focus in my prayer time to seek empathy and display the necessary balance of prophet and priest that is crucial for effective pastoral ministry. What did not change was my commitment to use the preaching moment to respond in real-time to real-life events and circumstances that affect the listening congregation spiritually and emotionally. Current event preaching is contextual preaching, which is to say every sermon is a current event sermon in one way or another. As the next chapter will show, the turbulent events of 2020 confirm this statement beyond what I could imagine.

Reflection Questions before You Preach

1. Am I trying to answer questions that I don't have the answer to?

2. Have I effectively connected the parallel lines between the biblical narrative and the current context?

3. Have I pointed the people toward hope by calling them to remembrance?

4. Am I calling the people to action, or simply calming them down?

5. What have I learned from past sermons I have preached that I can apply in this moment?

Notes

1. Leslie Callahan, "Neighborhood Watch," Samuel Dewitt Proctor Institute for Child Advocacy, Clinton, Tennessee, July 19, 2013, https://www.youtube.com/watch?v=-pjxpnVQvYg.

2. Ibid.

3. Renita J. Weems, "Scream," Riverside Church, New York City, February 20, 2015, https://www.youtube.com/watch?v=2gPB-w2XP5Y.

4. Otis Moss III, "A Word for Trayvon," Trinity United Church of Christ, Chicago, July 14, 2013, https://www.youtube.com/watch?v=X7FhMwHi-lE.

5. Weems.

6. Howard-John Wesley, "When the Verdict Hurts," Alfred Street Baptist Church, Alexandria, VA, July 14, 2013, https://www.youtube.com/watch?v=hqhOe85_vA8.

7. Ibid.

8. Marvin A. McMickle, *The Making of a Preacher: Five Essentials for Today's Ministers* (Valley Forge, PA: Judson Press, 2018), 8.

9. Frank A. Thomas, *How to Preach a Dangerous Sermon* (Nashville: Abingdon, 2018), 18.

10. Kenyatta Gilbert, *The Journey and Promise of African American Preaching* (Minneapolis: Fortress Press, 2011), 15.

11. Weems.

12. Wesley.

13. Ibid.

14. Ibid.

15. Wesley.

16. Moss.

17. Frank A. Thomas, *How to Preach a Dangerous Sermon* (Nashville: Abingdon, 2018), 18.

18. Ibid., 20.

19. Cleophas J. LaRue, *The Heart of Black Preaching* (Louisville, KY: Westminster John Knox, 2000), 10.

20. Wayne E. Croft Sr., *The Motif of Hope in African American Preaching during Slavery and the Post–Civil War Era* (Lanham, MD: Lexington Books, 2017), 1.

21. John S. McClure, *Preaching Words: 144 Key Terms in Homiletics* (Louisville, KY: Westminster John Knox, 2007), 117.

22. Croft, 18, quoting James H. Evans Jr., *We Have Been Believers: An African American Systematic Theology* (Minneapolis: Fortress Press, 1992).

23. Wesley.

24. Ibid.

25. Ibid.

26. Ibid.

27. Ibid.

28. Ibid.

29. Ibid.

30. James Weldon Johnson, "Lift Every Voice and Sing" (1900).

31. Wesley.

32. Noel L. Erskine, "Christian Hope and the Black Experience," *The Journal of Interdenominational Theological Center* 7, no. 1 (Fall 1979): 97.

33. Howard Thurman, *Jesus and the Disinherited* (New York: Abingdon, 1949), 69.

34. Wesley.

35. Ibid.

36. Ibid.

37. Callahan.

38. Ibid.

39. Callahan, quoting Martin Luther King Jr., "The Time to Break Silence."

40. Roger L. Ray, "Trayvon Is Dead and None of Us Are 'Not Guilty,'" The Emerging Church (formerly Community Christian Church), Springfield, MO, July 14, 2013, https://youtu.be/4BqDYwaMygA.

41. Ibid.

42. Ibid.

43. Callahan.

CHAPTER 6

May 31, 2020

Pentecost, When the World Is on Fire

The Perfect Storm

If Trayvon Martin's death represented the birth of the Black Lives Matter (BLM) movement, then the spring of 2020 is when it reached a fever pitch. The confluence of the COVID-19 pandemic resulting in a staggering loss of life worldwide, the rapid-fire succession of high-profile Black deaths at the hands of white law enforcement officers or civilians, a polarizing president in an election year, and pent-up frustrations from being quarantined at home during the most restrictive period of the pandemic resulted in a powder keg of protests and sometimes violent uprisings. It was a perfect storm of historic proportions. The deaths of Trayvon Martin, Mike Brown, and others gave rise to the movement, but the events of 2020 propelled BLM to become what the *New York Times* called "the largest civil rights movement in U.S. history."[1]

On February 23, 2020, around 1:00 p.m., Ahmaud Arbery, a twenty-five-year-old Black man, was murdered while jogging near his home outside of Brunswick, Georgia. Two white men armed with guns pursued Arbery in a pickup truck while a third man filmed the incident. The shooters claimed Arbery resembled a suspect in several neighborhood break-ins, though the neighborhood had only one burglary reported since January of that year—a handgun taken from an unlocked truck outside one of the suspect's homes. The shooting's immediate aftermath was a series of prose-cutors recusing themselves from the case because of an existing relationship with one of the suspects. There was an overall lack of action until the video of the incident surfaced in May of that year and began to circulate online. The suspects were finally arrested and charged on May 7—two and a half months after the incident, shortly before a fourth prosecutor took over the case.[2]

On March 13, 2020, Breonna Taylor, a twenty-six-year-old ER technician and former EMT, was fatally shot in her Louisville apart-ment by narcotics officers serving a no-knock warrant. Taylor's boyfriend initially fired at the officers thinking they were intruders, striking one in the leg. Officers responded with thirty-two shots, six of which hit Taylor, resulting in her death. The warrant was for indi-viduals who did not reside at her home, and after the shooting, the search was never executed. With the Arbery shooting in Georgia still fresh in the national news cycle, Taylor's death further amplified calls for justice amid unjust killings of African Americans. Taylor's profession as a first responder in the early days of the pandemic fur-ther magnified her case in the national spotlight. Unlike the Arbery case, Taylor's case had no video. The only charge in the case was for an officer who recklessly fired into a neighboring apartment, with no charges for the officer who killed Taylor.[3]

Of the high-profile deaths of African Americans at the hands of law enforcement or neighborhood vigilantes in the first half of 2020, the deaths of Arbery and Taylor contributed to the growing outrage. However, the murder of George Floyd by officer Derek Chauvin in Minneapolis was unquestionably the breaking point. On May 25, 2020, a store clerk called the Minneapolis police after suspecting that Floyd used a counterfeit twenty-dollar bill. Chauvin, one of the four arriving officers, subsequently subdued Floyd to the ground, holding his knee on Floyd's neck for more than nine minutes. The time was first believed to be eight minutes and forty-six seconds, inspiring worldwide protests for that length of time. "Die-ins" were staged where masses of people kneeled for eight minutes and forty-six seconds to symbolize the excess of Chauvin's brutality. However, further video evidence later came out showing that the amount of time Chauvin's knee was on Floyd's neck was longer, clocking in at nine minutes and twenty-nine seconds.[4]

What seared Floyd's death into the psyche of America was the release of the graphic video showing the entire crime in explicit detail. The world heard Floyd exclaiming, "I can't breathe" and crying for his mother for nearly five minutes. Then, we saw his body go lifeless while Chauvin kept his knee on his neck for nearly four more minutes.[5] The collective public trauma outraged even those not previously sympathetic to the BLM cause. The public murder of George Floyd and the viral video showing the gruesome detail impacted the BLM movement the same way Bloody Sunday on the Edmund Pettus Bridge in Selma had impacted the civil rights movement a generation before. The resulting protests immediately spread to more than two thousand communities large and small in more than sixty countries with millions participating in the demonstrations. Most protests were nonviolent; however, hundreds of cities experienced significant looting, arson, and property destruction. As buildings burned and National Guard troops descended upon cities, anger, fear, and frustration dominated the minds and hearts of anyone with a television, an Internet connection, or a window to look outside. This is what pastors faced as they prepared to preach the Sunday after.[6]

The Preaching Moment: Sunday, May 31
Pentecost, When the World Is on Fire

The Sunday after the murder of George Floyd was May 31, 2020—Pentecost Sunday. Pentecost is supposed to be a celebration of Christian unity, a commemoration of the birth of the church, a coming together of people from all nations under the power of the Holy Spirit, and a reversal of the confusion of Babel with clarity and understanding. But Pentecost Sunday 2020 was defined not by unity or understanding but by extreme polarization and rage. What began with an incident in Minneapolis had now incited worldwide outrage. Floyd died on Monday, May 25, and the first protests began the next day in Minneapolis. By the time Sunday came, the proverbial and literal fires had been raging for almost a week. Some of the most destructive riots occurred the night before on Saturday, May 30. My home, Philadelphia, was particularly hard hit by riots with rampant vandalism on the evening of May 30 into the early hours of May 31. Businesses and shopping centers across the city were looted and burned. Police and National Guard troops were unable to gain control. In this volatile context, pastors and preachers stood on Pentecost Sunday to speak a word from the Lord. What does it mean to preach the fire of the Holy Spirit on Pentecost in a city that is literally on fire?

The previous week's events were not the only thing that made that Sunday's preaching moment challenging. Sermons preached during this period in 2020 were especially unique because most churches were unable to meet in person due to COVID-19 protocols. Pastors were not only figuring out how to address historic, context-altering events in their sermons; they were also figuring out how to navigate preaching at all while congregations were unable to meet in person. Local pastors were instantly transformed into televangelists, preaching to cameras in empty rooms while parishioners watched on Facebook, Zoom, or YouTube. Those in the call-and-response tradition of the Black church were forced to navigate preaching in silence without the affirmation of "amens" to gauge effectiveness. The comforting fellowship of Sunday gathering was absent in a needed moment.

Additionally, that season was incredibly difficult because, beyond the preaching moment, the pandemic produced previously unseen trauma for pastors and congregants alike. While wrestling with the public deaths of Arbery, Taylor, and Floyd, churches and pastors were already grieving staggering sickness and deaths in their own numbers. Previously healthy members were contracting COVID-19 and expiring within a week with pastors unable to make hospital visits and unable to hold public funerals when they died. The loss of communal rituals of comfort and consolation added insult to injury. The immediate contextual concern was the aftermath of the George Floyd murder, but the pandemic remained the dominant concern that affected everyone's daily life. The two were in fact related to each other. By the week of May 25, the COVID lockdown had been in effect for more than two months. Parents were working from home while navigating online learning for children who were going to school at home. Movie theaters, clubs, and all social events including church gatherings were absent in favor of extreme social distancing measures. Restaurants and most stores other than supermarkets were closed. Many found themselves unemployed as entire industries were shuttered and decimated. Social distancing gave way to a social crisis. For many, the outrage over the Floyd murder ignited already pent-up frustrations, the result of which was explosive. Under these conditions, many pastors approached the preaching moment on Pentecost Sunday facing a camera in an empty room.

Dr. Clarence E. Wright, "Hollering at God" (Chosen 300 Ministries at Love Park, Philadelphia)

Sunday, May 31, 2020, is a preaching moment that I will never, ever forget. After watching the peaceful protests of the previous morning deteriorate into the chaos of the night before, I stood for two separate preaching engagements on the morning of May 31. The 9:00 a.m. engagement happened to be a previously scheduled outdoor service at Love Park in Center City Philadelphia. Love

Park is a frequent gathering place in the geographic center of town adjacent to Philadelphia City Hall. It also happens to be the site of some of the largest protests of the previous day and some of the worst destruction the previous night. It was a deceptively beautiful day with a warm spring breeze and the sky bright blue with minimal clouds. But as I arrived that morning to preach for a homeless outreach mission, I was greeted by National Guard troops stationed to protect City Hall and other municipal properties.

News cameras from every major station came to cover the destruction and cleanup efforts. A Starbucks next to City Hall had been burned down, and the charred remains of a police cruiser remained in the street. Some businesses had been boarded up. Others remained wide open, trashed, and relieved of their merchandise by looters, a few of whom were still going in and out to see what was left. A few blocks away on Chestnut Street, smoke was still rising from a large building the size of a city block that had been set ablaze overnight. This was the literal backdrop to my preaching, as I faced a crowd of homeless worshippers, volunteers preparing to serve a meal, curious passersby, and even more curious press cameras. I did not have to envision the social and cultural context that I was preaching to. It greeted me in the ashes of the burned police cruiser, the barrels of National Guard rifles, and the faces of all who came to hear a word.

At Love Park that morning, I preached a sermon entitled "Hollering at God." Like my 2013 sermon after the Zimmerman verdict, the text came from 2 Chronicles. This time, instead of the familiar "heal the land" text from 2 Chronicles 7:14, I meditated on 2 Chronicles 20:1-9 with emphasis on verse 9, which reads, "If calamity comes upon us, whether the sword of judgment, or plague or famine, we will stand in your presence before this temple that bears your Name and will cry out to you in our distress, and you will hear us and save us." That sermon opened by addressing the calamities that we were collectively facing in that moment and in conversation with the biblical text illustrating the importance of honesty in our prayers. Honesty and vulnerability together are the first of the four tasks of current event preaching, but that honesty should not be limited to the preaching voice. In distressing times, the listening congregation should also be empowered to be honest and vulnerable in their prayer lives. The tenor of the sermon pushed back at the notion that Christians should always look at the bright side of life and instead encouraged an authentic prayer life in which we "cry out to [God] in our distress."

Metaphoric parallelism is drawn from 2 Chronicles 20, where King Jehoshaphat faced the prospect of three nations that had joined together to wage war against him. Verse 3 notes that amid alarm his response was "to inquire of the LORD" and to proclaim a fast for all Judah. In the sermon, the three nations joining to wage war against Judah were juxtaposed with the three-headed monster of COVID-19, political instability, and state-sponsored violence against Black Americans. Prayer and fasting were not presented as an alternative to the stringent COVID-19 protocols, or as a substitute for and against protesting, marching, voting, or other tangible forms of fighting for justice. Prayer was affirmed as the spiritual exercise which should undergird all the other necessary responses. The tone of the prayer is what was especially emphasized:

> Somebody here today needs to know that God hears angry prayers!
> God hears you when you're hurting.
> God hears you when you're distressed.
> Sometimes your situation requires that you holler at God.
> And because God knows everything, God understands why you're angry.
> And I need to remind you that injustice angers God too!

When God sees God's people under attack, that makes God mad too!

When God sees someone with power, and privilege, and authority use it to harm someone they should be protecting, that makes God mad too!

So, when you go to God you might as well be real!

God doesn't want a fake prayer from you. God wants honesty!

Jehoshaphat's decision to pray and lead the people in prayer and fasting while facing an approaching calamity was presented as a call for prayer and fasting amid the parallel calamities of 2020. While the original narrative should maintain its unique character and historicity, it also informs our posture amid the metaphoric parallels of the contemporary context.

Prophetic remembrance toward hope is explicitly offered through a repetitive litany recalling various traumatic circumstances in history that African Americans have collectively survived by the hand of God:

If God brought us through the middle passage, God can bring us through right now.

If God brought us through chattel slavery, God can bring us through right now.

If God brought us through reconstruction, and sharecropping, and Jim Crow, God can bring us through right now.

If God brought us through the civil rights movement and the Black power movement, God can bring us through right now,

If God brought us through urban renewal, and the crack epidemic, and trickledown economics, God can bring us through right now.

If God brought us through "three strikes and you're
out" and mass incarceration, God can bring us through
right now,
    If we survived Reagan's economic policies, and Bush Sr.'s
war on drugs, and Bill Clinton's criminal justice reforms,
and Bush Jr.'s housing crisis, God can bring us through
right now!
    But we've got to come together and pray and fast, and
proclaim that God is our deliverer, God is our banner, God
is our strong tower!

Within this litany are several overtly political statements. While
intentionally bipartisan in criticism, invoking the names and (failed)
policies of Reagan, Clinton, and both Bushes during the darkest
days of the polarizing Trump presidency fulfills the prophetic task
of defining the terms of future hope based on remembrance of a
shared history. In this case, the hope is in survival to fight another
day. A decision to be apolitical is a decision to reject the prophetic
voice and preaching in general, and prophetic preaching particularly requires picking sides. As Lisa Thompson puts it, "Faith is not
neutral. Preaching is a practice of faith. Neutrality in preaching is
not attainable."[7] The choice to name the failed policies of previous
presidents by implication addressed the policies of the Trump
administration without ever mentioning his name. The overarching
point of naming failed policies of previous presidential administra-
tions was not to merely play the political blame game but to call to
remembrance the God who transcends even the worst policies and
gives those affected by them the power to survive and overcome.
    The final stanza of that litany transitions from prophetic
remembrance to the call to action, which was an invitation to
honest and passionate prayer. This call to action was embedded as
the main thesis throughout the sermon and emphasized in the sermonic close:

It may be hard to come to God right now. You may think you're too unstable, that you've got too many emotions to pray right now, but I'm here to tell you that God can handle it. The old folks used to say, "I came to him just as I was, weary, wounded, and sad, but I found in him a resting place, and he has made me glad." No matter what's going on, you can talk to God, you can cry to God, and yes, you can holler at God.

Dr. Clarence E. Wright, "I'm Mad, and So Is God" (Love Zion Baptist Church, Philadelphia)

The 9:00 a.m. service that day was also my first time preaching for a live crowd larger than twelve people in more than two months since services went online for COVID prevention. When I went to my home pulpit at the Love Zion Baptist Church, it was quite a different experience. Besides the present trauma following the murder of George Floyd and subsequent violent uprising, this was also on the heels of the worst period of the pandemic, long before vaccines were introduced and when people were dying by the thousands every day. Many legitimately feared for their lives. Amid a full shutdown of non-essential businesses and services, large indoor gatherings like worship services were deemed especially risky, and many churches including my own were still reeling from the sudden deaths of multiple members and the disruption of sacred routines. Churches employed many strategies for adaptation during the early months of the pandemic. Some shuttered their buildings with the pastor streaming worship services from home through a smartphone or tablet. Some invested in more advanced cameras and editing software for professionally produced prerecorded services. Some used Zoom for a more synchronous virtual experience. Others, like the church I serve, chose to broadcast from the sanctuary via social media using a small core team while the rest of the congregation watched from home.

Regulations in the city of Philadelphia at the time called for ten people or fewer gathered in an indoor space. At Love Zion, our core team consisted of four singers (a worship leader, soprano, alto, and tenor), two musicians, one minister, one deacon, one trustee, and me. Two media ministry workers were also present and vitally important, but they remained outside of the sanctuary in the lobby, which was converted into a makeshift production studio. This remained our setup for well over a year—twelve people in a sanctuary designed to hold more than three hundred. Even my own family stayed home and watched the service on the TV screen. This awaited me at the 11:00 a.m. service on May 31, 2020. Conversely, while only twelve people were in the church building, there were almost nine hundred views of that service across multiple web platforms—far more than we would ever have seen in Sunday attendance. But views on Facebook or YouTube could not begin to replace the warmth of a church hug or the cry of a baby during service. We all made the most of an unspeakably challenging situation, but the preaching environment often felt cold and empty, especially for those of us in the call-and-response tradition of the Black church. All of this made what already would have been an incredibly difficult preaching moment exponentially more challenging.

As a Baptist from a less liturgical tradition, I don't always stick to the Christian calendar when preparing sermons, but Pentecost is one of the exceptions. I am a proud member of what is colloquially known as the Bapticostal tradition, which are members of Baptist churches who affirm the continuation of spiritual gifts in the life of the church and have been heavily influenced by Pentecostalism. For me, Pentecost Sunday is an opportunity to remind my Baptist church that the story of the gospel does not end when Jesus "got up, early Sunday morning," but it continued fifty days later with the coming of the Holy Ghost at Pentecost. Pentecost is typically about the fellowship of believers, the signs and wonders of God, and the power to be witnesses for Christ. But while the sermon in 2020 was grounded in Acts 2, the Pentecost text, it had a decidedly different tone based on the context of the moment.

The sermon titled "I'm Mad, and So Is God" centered on the themes of unity, disruption, and fire drawn from the events and imagery of the day of Pentecost. Unlike the Sunday following the Zimmerman verdict seven years earlier, by May 2020, I was an experienced pastor. I had not only completed seminary, but two months prior, I had defended my doctoral thesis. I was keenly aware of the moment's importance and conscious of my less-than-stellar sermon seven years earlier. The thought of those "Negroes hearing about forgiveness and learning to be quiet" still echoed in my mind,[8] as did the four tasks of current event preaching. In many ways, "I'm Mad, and So Is God" was the culmination of three years of research and an opportunity to apply it.

Honesty and Vulnerability

The first task was to lose the veil of emotional stability and be honest about my true feelings. After the Trayvon verdict, I felt responsible for calming and pacifying emotions. I feared that leaning into the anger would escalate a turbulent situation and potentially cause riots or other violence. After George Floyd's death, however, the violence, riots, and outrage had already occurred. I had learned my lesson about pretension and emotion policing, but I was also keenly aware that the proverbial bubble had already busted. My task was neither to prevent a riot nor chastise those who may have participated in them, but rather to begin the process of healing by incarnationally expressing my own anger and walking together through the valley with both the people and our empathetic God. The first words of the sermon immediately expressed honesty and vulnerability:

To be honest with you, I'm not feeling particularly pastoral right now. Like many of you, I have been dealing with a range of emotions since watching Derek Chauvin, a white police officer, kneel on George Floyd's neck until he died. The truth is, like many of you, I'm angry that yet another Black man has been murdered by someone sworn to protect him. I'm frustrated by the delay in justice whenever the perpetrator is a police officer. I'm overwhelmed by the fact that while police are killing Black folks, COVID-19 is still killing Black folks disproportionately, and members of our own communities are still killing each other.

"I'm not feeling particularly pastoral right now" echoes Howard-John Wesley's putting down the "Reverend Doctor" in favor of the "Howard-John."[9] This expression of vulnerability at the beginning of the sermon sets the tone as conversational rather than the authoritative voice of the pastor proclaiming the Word of God. This is as much a theological statement as it is a preaching technique. If God is incarnational and chooses to dwell with us amid our stresses and sorrows, then we ought to follow God's model. Preachers have no reason to appear to be above it when even God is in it.

Prophetic Remembrance toward Hope

Sometimes honesty contradicts hope. During prophetic remembrance, hope is not always immediate. Hope must be built, and sometimes it first requires a period of healthy lament. In this sermon, there was much lament, notably expressed in a litany of previous deaths during the BLM movement, none of which resulted in a conviction:

> While I'm supposed to be encouraging you that it gets better and it's gonna be all right, I remember that Trayvon

Martin is dead, and George Zimmerman is a free man today.

I remember that Michael Brown is dead, and Darren Wilson is a free man today.

Philando Castile is dead; Jeronimo Yanez is a free man today.

Freddie Gray is dead, and the six officers who caused his death are free today.

Terence Crutcher is dead; Betty Jo Shelby is free today.

Alton Sterling is dead; Howie Lake and Blane Salamoni are free today.

Tamir Rice is dead; Timothy Loehmann is free today.

Eric Garner is dead; Daniel Pantaleo is free today and was allowed to remain on the police force, five years after he choked Garner to death.

And now, six years after Eric Garner was killed, we still can't breathe! . . .

Yet, even in the midst of tragedy, death, and violence, I'm reminded that all hope is not lost.

Even in moments like this, when it feels hopeless, there is a bright side somewhere!

Admittedly, in the BLM age, reading a long list of names has become so commonplace that it borders on cliché. The hashtags #sayhisname and #sayhername have become synonymous with the movement. The preaching community has been no exception to this, but the lists of names can be problematic if included as an afterthought or added on to make a standard sermon appear to be socially conscious or justice oriented. Listing names gratuitously can even appear exploitative when misused. I have seen more than a few sermons invoke the names of Trayvon, Mike Brown, Sandra Bland, and more as a cheap grab for amens from a congregation they perceive as social justice oriented. Prophetic remembrance may not always start with hope, but it should always be pointed in that direction. Outrage is never the goal of preaching; hope, justice, and love are. Outrage is a tool to inspire action, but hope paints the picture of what justice looks like.

I included a list of names to contextualize the tangible outrage of that moment. The anger that I believed that members of my congregation felt, and that protesters and rioters all felt, was not an isolated response to George Floyd. It had been building up through years of Black death and a complete lack of accountability. On May 31, 2020, that list of names was relevant to the tumultuous events that precipitated the preaching moment. To state the theme "I'm mad, and so is God" required an explanation of the anger's source. But the preacher must be sure not to get stuck in the place of anger and despair. Honesty is necessary, even when it includes anger, but the goal of the preaching moment remains hope for the hopeless. In this case, hope begins with "yet." In the Black preaching tradition, "yet" or "but" is a powerful conjunction—no matter what comes before, there is always hope after!

Metaphoric Parallelism

This sermon provides several examples of metaphoric parallelism, one of which stems from the unity of language on the day of Pentecost. The need for understanding is at the root of every protest or movement for justice. For the systemically marginalized or oppressed, acts of nonviolent protest and sometimes destructive riots are both efforts to be understood. They are a call for attention to matters of injustice that are invisible to those not affected by them. Movements for justice and equality are driven by publicity. Publicity shifts the marginalized to the center. Through publicity, the invisible becomes seen and the voice of the unheard becomes valued and ultimately understood. The interpretive miracle of Pentecost was used to metaphorically point to the need for understanding after the murder of George Floyd:

The tongues on the day of Pentecost were not of a confusing or ecstatic nature but of clarity.

Unity in language is a sign of understanding.

Unity of language is one of the markers of community.

And out of the chaos of Pentecost came a community that could understand each other.

To function as a community, we have to understand each other.

The events of this week show that we as a people just want to be understood.

Martin Luther King Jr. famously said, "A riot is the language of the unheard," although that soundbite is often misappropriated from the original meaning. King was ideologically nonviolent. His intention was never to condone violence, looting, or property destruction. He was merely pointing out that condemning the rioters is not enough. On one of several occasions in 1966 where he said this, he continued:

> And what is it that America has failed to hear? It has failed to hear that the plight of the Negro poor has worsened over the last few years. It has failed to hear that the promises of freedom and justice have not been met. And it has failed to hear that large segments of white society are more concerned about tranquility and the status quo than about justice, equality, and humanity. And so in a real sense our nation's summers of riots are caused by our nation's winters of delay.[10]

More than fifty years after King's quote about riots and the unheard, in the wake of the worst rioting in a generation, I invited the listening congregation to ask the question, "In the aftermath of state-sponsored death and oppression, when we see destruction in our cities what are they really trying to say." Pentecost is an invitation to hear those who were previously unheard, and that is the work of the Holy Spirit.

Call to Action

The call to action drawn from the Pentecost narrative was threefold: unity, disruption, and the fire. Together these three comprised the major points of the sermon. Unity, the first call to action, is an important part of the Pentecost narrative. The notion of being "with one accord in one place," as the classic King James Version renders it, is a central component of the text. However, this presented a contextual challenge while in a virtual service and observing strict social distancing protocols. What does it mean to be "all together in one place" when we are not physically together in one place but scattered from house to house? A call for unity while quarantined in separate houses requires a deeper look at what it means to be together. While physical proximity was certainly a component of the day of Pentecost in Acts, the context of 2020 required new questions to be asked and a new approach to Christian unity:

> On the surface, the verse appears to highlight physical proximity. The same physical proximity that we're unable to participate in because of COVID-19 protocols. A focus on physical proximity challenges the nature of this very worship service that we're in right now. How can we have Pentecost when we're scattered from house to house and neighborhood to neighborhood? How can the wind of God meet us in "one place" when we're not in "one place"? How can the glory of the Spirit move through the crowd when there is no crowd, just a skeleton crew of ten people trying to keep worship going? But the words "one place" don't represent the thematic thrust of this verse, but rather the word that comes before, which is "together."

The burning questions were asked and answered through the biblical text in a way that addressed the current situation. The major implication for a church and world that were forcibly separated as a life-saving measure was that you don't have to be physically together to be together. "Together" indicates mindset, purpose, and focus even when physical proximity is not possible.

The second call to action was disruption. The pursuit of justice and righteousness often requires shaking up the status quo. At its core, that is what the BLM movement has been—a disruption of the status quo. With this as a backdrop, the Holy Spirit in Acts 2 is presented as a disrupter. Likewise, the listening congregants are invited as followers of God to break out of various comfort zones and disrupt the status quo.

Finally, "the fire" is presented as both metaphoric parallelism and a call to action. The fire in Acts 2 is presented as a symbol of power. In conversation with James Baldwin's *The Fire Next Time*,[11] the fire of the spirit in Acts 2 is juxtaposed with the fires of protest that burned the night before. Ultimately, a line of distinction was drawn between getting struct by fire and getting filled with fire:

> There is a difference between getting struck by fire and getting filled with fire!
>
> When you're struck by fire, you are on the wrong side of an angry God.
>
> When you're struck by fire, you are the cause of God's anger and therefore stand to be judged.
>
> When you're struck by fire, you burn and are consumed.
>
> When you're struck by fire, God is fighting you.
>
> But when you're filled with fire, God is joining you in the fight!

Together the call for unity, disruption, and fire are each drawn from Acts 2 but are presented as parallels to the turbulent events of the previous week. Each served as an invitation to continue the fight for justice while always being led by the Spirit.

Peter and the Original Pentecost Sermon

"I'm Mad, and So Is God" could rightfully be described as an angry sermon. Even the title makes this apparent. Likewise, Peter's original Pentecost sermon could also be described as an angry sermon, and it was preached following another public, state-sponsored killing of a man from a marginalized community. Through this lens, Jesus and George Floyd have very similar stories, and the significance of the Sunday after falling on Pentecost is profound. Pentecost Sunday in 2020 was an echo of the original Pentecost. The sociopolitical environment was similarly unstable, and a movement was birthed after a public execution. There has always been power and possibility amid the chaos of Pentecost, and preachers will continue to stand in the fire to bring hope in perilous times as Peter did on that inaugural Pentecost.

In Acts 2:14-16, Peter raised his voice and addressed the crowd as "fellow Jews and all of you who live in Jerusalem." He told them to listen carefully to what he had to say and proceeded to explain the unexplainable. He explained that the people were not drunk and that it was the fulfillment of a prophecy from the prophet Joel, and he took his text from Joel 2:28-32. In his explanation of that prophecy, Peter showed that the power received on Pentecost was available to all; "sons and daughters," "men and women" (all genders), old men and young men (all ages), Jews and converts to Judaism (all cultures and all faiths). Verse 21 spells it out explicitly: "Everyone who calls on the name of the Lord will be saved." Because the crowd was so vast, he had to preach an inclusive message. He couldn't preach to thousands of people from all over the world in the same way he preached to a small group of Galileans. His chosen text and delivery were both strategically inclusive.

Peter's preaching strategy also serves as a lesson for today's virtual age of preaching. Peter had a multinational, multiethnic, multicultural audience because they were gathered from all over the known world to observe Pentecost. Today, with the Internet and social media, local sermons are no longer local. By pressing a button that says, "go live," there is instantly worldwide access to our local worship assemblies. I was shocked in the early days of virtual worship during the pandemic to discover that not only had our views skyrocketed, but they were coming from all over the world. Africa, Europe, Asia, and South America—places I had visited for short-term mission trips—could now hear me preach from my local North Philadelphia pulpit. May 31, 2020, echoed the original Pentecost in more ways than one.

In verses 22-24, Peter made it known who Jesus was. He reminded them that Jesus was accredited by God through the miracles, wonders, and signs that he performed, but in verse 23 Peter gets personal. He tells the crowd point blank: Jesus was handed over to "you." He said "you," with the help of wicked men, put him to death by nailing him to the cross. This was not a message to make the crowd feel good. It was an accusatory message. Peter wasn't trying to endear himself to the crowd; he was trying to make them see the error of their ways. With the words of his sermon, Peter was implicating the entire crowd in the death of Jesus. We have only the words of Scripture. We don't have a recording of this sermon to examine Peter's intonation or body language, but it sounds like an angry sermon. It's hard to imagine that less than two months removed from the events of Maundy Thursday and Good Friday, Peter did not still bear some emotional scars from seeing Jesus arrested, tortured, and crucified. Surely Peter, who was prone to violence and lacked impulse control, was emotional in his sermonic delivery. Surely the man with documented anger issues was not calm and collected while retelling the events of Jesus's crucifixion. The resurrection reversed the power of death and the grave, but it did not erase the memory of those who witnessed it. In verse 24, Peter preaches the gospel of the resurrection when he tells them that even though you killed him, "God raised him from the dead . . . because it was impossible for death to keep its hold on him." Peter preached the hope of the resurrection, but he remembered the trauma of the crucifixion.

Peter continued to make his claim of Jesus as Messiah using Psalm 16:8-11 as a supporting text, finally stating in verses 32-33, "God raised this Jesus to life, and we are all witnesses of it. Exalted to the right hand of God, he has received from the Father the promised Holy Spirit and has poured out what you now see and hear." The words "what you now see and hear" are Peter contextualizing the Scripture in the moment. By verse 36, Peter is ready for his dramatic conclusion. He said, "Therefore let all Israel be assured of this: God has made this Jesus, whom you crucified, both Lord and Messiah." This was Peter's mic drop moment—the summative statement of his thesis—followed by the most significant altar call in history. And with that, the church was born. Even in his final statement, while declaring the power of the resurrection and the lordship of Jesus the Messiah, Peter still maintained an accusatory tone: "this Jesus, whom you crucified," proving that even an angry sermon can have a lasting impact.

Peter preached the resurrection of Christ while still remembering his crucifixion. It is not a stretch to see George Floyd as a type of Christ in the allegorical sense. He certainly should not be deified or worshipped like the blameless Son of God, but on a human level, his death and the movement which he inspired are quite familiar. In *The Cross and the Lynching Tree*, James H. Cone drew a parallel between the Roman cross of first-century Jerusalem and the lynching tree of twentieth-century America. Though the instrument of death was a knee and not a tree, the murder of George Floyd bears striking similarities to the dark history of lynching in America. Cone says, "Until we can see the cross and the lynching tree together, until we can identify Christ with a 'recrucified' Black body hanging from a lynching tree, there can be no genuine understanding of Christian identity in America, and no deliverance from the brutal legacy of slavery and white supremacy."[12] Sadly, a decade after Cone wrote those words, the proverbial lynching tree is still bearing strange fruit. Nevertheless, the task of the preacher is not merely to highlight the present trials and traumas or to dwell in the anger, but to lift the listening congregation to action, to hope, and ultimately to joy.

Reflection Questions before You Preach

1. Have I been honest in my prayers of preparation?

2. What environmental factors should I consider and adapt my sermon delivery to?

3. Is there a significant occasion on the secular or Christian calendar that coincides with the current moment?

4. Am I seeking to be neutral, or faithfully leading people to take the side of righteousness?

5. What have I learned from past sermons I have preached that I can apply in this moment?

Notes

1. Larry Buchanan, Quoctrung Bui, and Jugal K. Patel, "Black Lives Matter May Be the Largest Movement in US History," *New York Times*, July 3, 2020, https://www.nytimes.com/interactive/2020/07/03/us/george-floyd-protests-crowd-size.html.

2. Richard Fausset, Michael Levenson, Sarah Mervosh, and Derrick Bryson Taylor, "Ahmaud Arbery Shooting: A Timeline of the Case," *New York Times*, February 22, 2022, https://www.nytimes.com/article/ahmaud-arbery-timeline.html.

3. Malachy Browne, Anjali Singhvi, Natalie Reneau, and Drew Jordan, "How the Police Killed Breonna Taylor," *New York Times*, December 28, 2020, https://www.nytimes.com/video/us/100000007348445/breonna-taylor-death-cops.html.

4. Eric Levenson, "Former Officer Knelt on George Floyd for 9 Minutes and 29 Seconds—Not the Infamous 8:46," CNN, March 30, 2021, https://www.cnn.com/2021/03/29/us/george-floyd-timing-929-846/index.html.

5. Ibid.

6. Audra D. S. Burch, Weiyi Cai, Gabriel Gianordoli, Morrigan McCarthy, and Jugal K. Patel, "How Black Lives Matter Reached Every Corner of America," *New York Times*, June 13, 2020, https://www.nytimes.com/interactive/2020/06/13/us/george-floyd-protests-cities-photos.html.

7. Lisa L. Thompson, *Preaching the Headlines: Possibilities and Pitfalls* (Minneapolis: Fortress Press, 2021), 11.

8. Leslie Callahan, "Neighborhood Watch," Samuel Dewitt Proctor Institute for Child Advocacy, Clinton, Tennessee, July 19, 2013, https://www.youtube.com/watch?v=-pjxpnVQvYg.

9. Howard-John Wesley, "When the Verdict Hurts," Alfred Street Baptist Church, Alexandria, Virginia, July 14, 2013, https://www.youtube.com/watch?v=hqhOe85_vA8.

10. Lily Rothman, "What Martin Luther King Really Thought About Riots," *Time*, April 28, 2015, https://time.com/3838515/baltimore-riots-language-unheard-quote/.

11. James Baldwin, *The Fire Next Time* (New York: The Dial Press, 1963).

12. James H. Cone, *The Cross and the Lynching Tree* (Maryknoll, NY: Orbis Books, 2011), 17.

Conclusion:
The Celebratory Close
Black Joy in the Midst of Black Pain

An Overwhelming Black Joy

In 2015, I attended the Brave New Voices (BNV) poetry festival in Atlanta as a workshop presenter. BNV is a weeklong international gathering of youth poets featuring classes, performances, and a slam competition to determine a champion team. That year on the final stage the Philadelphia Youth Poetry Movement (PYPM) team performed a poem titled "Glory." That poem that highlighted the power of Black joy was particularly profound because, as is common in youth poetry slams, the subject matter of the performances up until that point was largely serious and sometimes traumatic. Performance poetry is a largely cathartic exercise, particularly among youth learning to process grief and trauma, so issues of racism, abandonment, sexual assault, and mental illness are common in the poems presented. Performers are given space to work through those issues in the form of beautiful spoken art and celebrated for their bravery. Nevertheless, four rounds of four teams with triggering topic after triggering topic can be emotionally taxing on the performers and listening audience alike. Enter the PYPM team, who despite high scores for previous poems with serious subject matters decided to perform "Glory."

The poem began with a similarly somber tone before a dramatic volta that opened the floodgates for the joyous. The opening line, "I've been watching Black bodies blend into the pavement for some time now . . . but have not lost hope,"[1] epitomizes the notion of Black joy as an act of resistance. Poet Toi Derricotte is credited with coining the phrase "Joy is an act of resistance" from her poem series titled "The Telly Cycle."[2] But it was that performance by the youth poetry team from Philadelphia when I was exposed to this concept, and it ignited something within me. Those four teenagers on that stage describe Black joy as "an uncompromising revolution."[3] In the year after Tamir Rice was killed, after Mike Brown lay lifeless on the streets of Ferguson, and months after Baltimore erupted in violence following the death of Freddie Gray, the youth from Philadelphia declared, "We are calling for an overwhelming Black joy."[4]

I took those words to heart that day in 2015. In the years since, I have been deliberate in celebrating and highlighting Black joy as an act of resistance to the perils of these turbulent times. In the process, I have found new energy to wrestle with the issues of our time. Brittney Cooper sums it up best: "Maintaining the capacity for joy is critical to the struggle for justice."[5] I have certainly not given up other necessary forms of protest, nor expressing anger when it is called for, but the notion of joy as a revolutionary act was freeing. While it was a poetry slam that jump-started my own dedication to the revolution of Black joy, the notion of joy in the face of pain has long been a hallmark of Black preaching. The role of recovering joy during the Black Lives Matter (BLM) movement is further evidence that, despite its secular façade, BLM has been inherently spiritual at its core, heavily influenced by the Black church even if not led by it.

We Gon' Be Alright

The last line of that PYPM poem sent the crowd into a jubilant response with four simple but profound words: "We gon' be alright." Those words come from the hook of a song titled "Alright" by hip-hop artist Kendrick Lamar that became an anthem for the BLM movement after the deaths of Mike Brown in Ferguson, Missouri, Tamir Rice in Cleveland, Ohio, and Freddie Gray in Baltimore, Maryland, among others in the year prior. The song was released in 2015 as the fourth single from Lamar's album *To Pimp a Butterfly*. It gained attention that year after the BET awards because Lamar performed it on top of a vandalized police car, as a visual representation of unrest in Ferguson that year. While the verses of the song contain some controversial lyrics, notably "We hate po' po' wanna kill us dead in the streets fo sho" (po' po' being a reference to police),[6] the overall theme was Black joy in the face of Black death and trauma. The juxtaposition of the verses detailing the struggle for Black survival with the chorus triumphantly declaring that "we gon' be alright" propelled the song to be a hit on the music charts and radio and the soundtrack of many national protests. In between chants of "No justice, no peace, no racist police," crowds of demonstrators would break out in the chorus of "We Gon' Be Alright" the way their parents and grandparents sang "We Shall Overcome" fifty years prior. The centrality of a hip-hop artist like Kendrick Lamar compared with the bellowing gospel tone of Mahalia Jackson in the civil rights era speaks to the secular roots of BLM as a movement, but while stylistically worlds apart, Lamar's core message remains the same. The phrase "If God got us then we gon' be alright" is an inherently gospel message and illustrates the spiritual heartbeat of the movement despite not being overtly Christian in its application.[7]

The protesters chanting, "We gon' be alright" broken up by the rhythmic response of "Eh!" is merely a generational reinterpretation of what gospel legend Shirley Caesar sang forty years prior: "This joy that I have, the world didn't give it to me, the world didn't give it to me, the world can't take it away!"[8] This expression of hope and resilience has long been a hallmark of Black faith and by extension Black preaching. The presence of joy has never been situational in the Black church. Joy has always been a ubiquitous presence in the Black church through slavery, Jim Crow, generational poverty, community violence, and more. The joy of the Lord has never been dependent on present circumstances. In the culture of Black Christianity, a church without joy is a problem, incomplete, like a car without wheels or a house with no roof. Whether in a demonstrative Pentecostal dance or the solemn liturgy of a Black Catholic, the joy of the Lord is the result of worship in a community of faith. Lament has its role, but if we come to church and there is no joy, we're doing it wrong! This is the crucial role of celebration in the preaching moment—to be a bridge from the cares of this world to the joy of the Lord.

Come Celebrate with Me

Poet Lucille Clifton best summarizes the essence of Black joy when she writes, "Come celebrate with me that every day something has tried to kill me and has failed."[9] This striking closing line of her poem, "come celebrate with me," illustrates the spiritual act of resilience in which preachers lead congregations from despair to joy. Henry Mitchell provided a window to the importance of celebration in Black preaching in his groundbreaking work *Celebration and Experience in Preaching.* In Mitchell's words, "The genius of Black preaching has been its capacity to generate celebration despite circumstances."[10] Black preaching is known for its celebratory close, but the musical and rhythmic conclusion of many sermons in the Black preaching tradition (or "whoop," as it's known) is not a mere stylistic choice or cultural expression. It is a profound theological statement. The whoop is the personification of the celebration despite the cares of the world. In short, the celebratory close is a profound display of Black joy as an act of resistance. But the celebration must first be evoked through the faithful delivery of hope. Wayne Croft says, "In the Black preaching tradition, a dimension of hope evokes celebration. Hope, thus, is evidenced in celebration, and celebration is rooted in hope."[11]

Joy is the natural result of the hope given through the preached word. The joy that comes at the end of the sermon proceeds from the hope that has been offered by reconciling the biblical text with the present cares of the world. In other words, you earn your whoop by giving hope. Without hope, there is no celebration. But preaching must give more than a reason to celebrate amid challenging circumstances—it must also give the means to lift out of those circumstances. In the words of Mitchell, "The sermon that celebrates without giving help is an opiate. The sermon that tries to help without celebration is, at least in the Black church, ineffective."[12] Preaching in this moment and the moments to come means inspiring hope while motivating to action. To be effective, one cannot happen without the other.

Notes

1. "Glory," performed by Philadelphia Youth Poetry Movement (PYPM), Brave New Voices Poetry Festival, Atlanta, GA, 2015, https://www.youtube.com/watch?v=ICBPUX4922Q.

2. Toi Derricotte, "The Telly Cycle," from Rattle #31 Tribute to African American Poets, June 2009.

3. PYPM.

4. Ibid.

5. Brittney Cooper, *Eloquent Rage: A Black Feminist Discovers Her Superpower* (London: Picador, 2018).

6. Kendrick Lamar, "Alright," track 7 on *To Pimp a Butterfly*, compact disc, Aftermath/Interscope, 2015.

7. Ibid.

8. Shirley Caesar, "The World Didn't Give It to Me," track 6 on *Be Careful of the Stones You Throw*, HOB Records, 1975.

9. Lucille Clifton, "Won't You Celebrate with Me," in *Book of Light* (Port Townsend, WA: Copper Canyon Press, 1993).

10. Henry H. Mitchell, *Celebration and Experience in Preaching* (Nashville: Abingdon, 1990), 12.

11. Wayne E. Croft Sr., *The Motif of Hope in African American Preaching during Slavery and the Post–Civil War Era* (Lanham, MD: Lexington Books, 2017), 118.

12. Mitchell, 131.

Bibliography

Albrecht, Gloria H. *The Character of Our Communities: Toward an Ethic of Liberation for the Church*. Nashville: Abingdon, 1995.

Alexander, Michelle. *The New Jim Crow: Mass Incarceration in the Age of Colorblindness*. New York: The New Press, 2012.

Almasy, Steve. "Trayvon's Dad: My Heart Is Broken, My Faith Is Not." CNN, July 15, 2013. https://www.cnn.com/2013/07/13/us/zimmerman-martin-family-reaction/index.html.

Allen, O. Wesley, Jr. *Preaching and the Human Condition: Loving God, Self, and Others*. Nashville: Abingdon, 2016.

———. *Preaching in the Era of Trump*. Danvers, MA: Chalice Press, 2017.

Alvarez, Lizette, and Cara Buckley. "Zimmerman Is Acquitted in Trayvon Martin Killing." *New York Times*, July 13, 2013. https://www.nytimes.com/2013/07/14/us/george-zimmerman-verdict-trayvon-martin.html.

Baldwin, James. *The Fire Next Time*. New York: The Dial Press, 1963.

Boggs, Donald (director). "A Ripple of Hope." Documentary. Covenant Productions, 2008.

Browne, Malachy, Anjali Singhvi, Natalie Reneau, and Drew Jordan. "How the Police Killed Breonna Taylor." *New York Times*, December 28, 2020. https://www.nytimes.com/video/us/100000007348445/breonna-taylor-death-cops.html.

Brueggemann, Walter. *The Prophetic Imagination*. Philadelphia: Fortress Press, 1978.

Buchanan, Larry, Quoctrung Bui, and Jugal K. Patel. "Black Lives Matter May Be the Largest Movement in US History." *New York Times*, July 3, 2020. https://www.nytimes.com/interactive/2020/07/03/us/george-floyd-protests-crowd-size.html.

Burch, Audra D. S., Weiyi Cai, Gabriel Gianordoli, Morrigan McCarthy, and Jugal K. Patel. "How Black Lives Matter Reached Every Corner of America." *New York Times*, June 13, 2020. https://www.nytimes.com/interactive/2020/06/13/us/george-floyd-protests-cities-photos.html.

Caesar, Shirley. "The World Didn't Give It to Me." Track 6 on *Be Careful of the Stones You Throw*. HOB Records, 1975.

Callahan, Leslie. "Neighborhood Watch." Samuel Dewitt Proctor Institute for Child Advocacy, Clinton, Tennessee, July 19, 2013. https://www.youtube.com/watch?v=-pjxpnVQvYg.

Carey, Mittie K. "The Freedom Faith Speeches of Prathia L. Hall: Uncovering a Hybrid Rhetoric of Protest." PhD diss., Baylor University, 2011.

Clifton, Lucille. "Won't You Celebrate with Me." In *Book of Light*. Port Townsend, WA: Copper Canyon Press, 1993.

Coates, Ta-Nehisi. *Between the World and Me*. New York: Spiegel & Grau, 2015.

Cone, James H. *Black Theology and Black Power*. New York: Seabury Press, 1969; reprint ed., Maryknoll, NY: Orbis Books, 2005.

———. *The Cross and the Lynching Tree*. Maryknoll, NY: Orbis Books, 2011.

Cooper, Brittney. *Eloquent Rage: A Black Feminist Discovers Her Superpower*. London: Picador, 2018.

Croft, Wayne E., Sr. *The Motif of Hope in African American Preaching during Slavery and the Post–Civil War Era*. Lanham, MD: Lexington Books, 2017.

Dawn, Randee, and Susan Green. *The Law & Order: SVU Unofficial Companion*. Dallas: BenBella Books, 2009.

———. "Ripped from the Headlines." *New York Times*, May 21, 2010. http://www.nytimes.com/slideshow/2010/05/21/ny region/20100523-ripped-slideshow/s/20100523-ripped-slideshow-slide-4AX4.html.

Derricotte, Toi. "The Telly Cycle." Rattle #31 Tribute to African American Poets, June 2009.

Dias, Elizabeth. "The Best Sermon About Trayvon That You Will Hear." *Time*, July 18, 2013. http://swampland.time.com/2013 /07/18/the-best-sermon-about-trayvon-that-you-will-hear/.

Douglass, Frederick. *Life and Times of Frederick Douglass.* Revised ed., 1892; reprint ed., New York: Collier, 1962.

Dunne, Peter Finley. *Observations by Mr. Dooley.* New York: Harper and Brothers, 1906.

Erskine, Noel L. "Christian Hope and the Black Experience." *The Journal of Interdenominational Theological Center* 7, no. 1 (Fall 1979): 88–100.

Evans, James H., Jr. *We Have Been Believers: An African American Systematic Theology.* Minneapolis: Fortress Press, 1992.

Fausset, Richard, Mervosh Levenson, Sarah Michael, and Derrick Bryson Taylor. "Ahmaud Arbery Shooting: A Timeline of the Case." *New York Times*, February 22, 2022. https://www.nytimes.com/article/ahmaud-arbery-timeline.html.

Flowers, Andy. "Five Reasons Not to Preach About Current Events." *Transformed: Living the Gospel in an Everyday World* (blog), Western Seminary, September 27, 2017. https://web.archive .org/web/20211016140642/https://transformedblog.westernsemi- nary.edu/2017/09/27/5-reasons-not-preach-current-events/

Fuller, Scott. "Sermon Tips: Current Events and When the Regular Sermon Just Won't Do." Pittsburgh Theological Seminary, August 20, 2015. https://www.pts.edu/blog/sermon-tips-current events/.

Fulton, Sabrina. @SybrinaFulton. "Lord during my darkest hour I lean on you. You are all that I have. At the end of the day, GOD is still in control. Thank you all for your prayers and support. I will love you forever Trayvon!!! In the name of Jesus!!!" Twitter, July 13, 2013. https://twitter.com/SybrinaFulton/status/356248501 421735936.

————. @SybrinaFulton. "I would like to share with you my favorite bible verse: Trust in the Lord with all your heart and lean not on your own understanding; in all your ways submit to him, and he will make your paths straight. Proverbs 3:5-6 What's your favorite Bible Verse?" Twitter, July 13, 2013. https://twitter .com/SybrinaFulton/status/356042681362817026.

————, and Tracy Martin. *Rest in Power: A Parents' Story of Love, Injustice, and the Birth of a Movement*. New York: Spiegel & Grau, 2017.

Gilbert, Kenyatta. *The Journey and Promise of African American Preaching*. Minneapolis: Fortress Press, 2011.

"Glory." Performed by Philadelphia Youth Poetry Movement (PYPM). Brave New Voices Poetry Festival, Atlanta, Georgia, 2015. https://www.youtube.com/watch?v=ICBPUX4922Q.

Gutiérrez, Gustavo. *A Theology of Liberation: History, Politics, and Salvation*. Maryknoll, NY: Orbis Books, 1973.

Hall, Prathia. "Between the Wilderness and the Cliff." *The African American Pulpit* 10, no. 9 (Summer 2007): 44–48.

"Herstory." July 5, 2019. https://blacklivesmatter.com/ about/herstory/.

Jones, Miles. *Preaching Papers: The Hampton and Virginia Union Lectures*. New York: Martin Luther King Fellows Press, 1995.

Johnson, James Weldon. "Lift Every Voice and Sing." Public domain hymn, 1900.

King, Martin Luther, Jr. "Beyond Vietnam: A Time to Break Silence." Riverside Church, New York City, April 4, 1967. http://rcha.rutgers.edu/images/2016-2017/1960s/Documents/7.-RCHA-2016-The-Culture-of-the-Sixties-Martin-Luther-King-Jr.-Beyond-Vietnam-condensed.pdf.

————. "I Have a Dream." March on Washington for Jobs and Freedom, Washington, DC, August 28, 1963.

————. *Strength to Love*. Cleveland: Collins & World, 1963.

Lamar, Kendrick. "Alright." Track 7 on *To Pimp a Butterfly*. Compact disc. Aftermath/Interscope, 2015.

LaRue, Cleophas J. *The Heart of Black Preaching*. Louisville, KY: Westminster John Knox, 2000.

Lederach, John Paul. *The Moral Imagination: The Art and Soul of Building Peace*. New York: Oxford University Press, 2005.

Levenson, Eric. "Former Officer Knelt on George Floyd for 9 Minutes and 29 Seconds—Not the Infamous 8:46." CNN, March 30, 2021. https://www.cnn.com/2021/03/29/us/george-floyd-timing-929-846/index.html.

Long, Thomas G. *The Witness of Preaching*. Louisville, KY: Westminster John Knox, 2003.

Marx, Karl. *Critique of Hegel's Philosophy of Right*. 1843.

Becker, Ron, Nick Marx, and Matt Sienkiewicz, eds. *Saturday Night Live and American TV*. Bloomington: Indiana University Press, 2013.

Martin, Tracy. @BTraymartin9. "Even though I am broken hearted my faith is unshattered I WILL ALWAYS LOVE MY BABY TRAY." Twitter, July 12, 2013. https://twitter.com/BTraymartin9/status/356238887158431747.

Matthews, Victor H. *The Hebrew Prophets and Their Social World*. Grand Rapids, MI: Baker Academic, 2012.

McClain, William B. *Come Sunday: The Liturgy of Zion*. Nashville: Abingdon, 1990.

McClure, John S. *Preaching Words: 144 Key Terms in Homiletics*. Louisville, KY: Westminster John Knox, 2007.

McMickle, Marvin A. *Be My Witness: The Great Commission for Preachers*. Valley Forge, PA: Judson Press, 2016.

———. *The Making of a Preacher: Five Essentials for Today's Ministers*. Valley Forge, PA: Judson Press, 2018.

Mitchell, Henry H. *Celebration and Experience in Preaching*. Nashville: Abingdon, 1990.

Moltmann, Jürgen. *Theology of Hope: On the Ground and the*

Implications of a Christian Eschatology. New York: Harper & Row, 1967.

Moss, Otis, III. *Blue Note Preaching in a Post-Soul World: Finding Hope in an Age of Despair.* Louisville, KY: Westminster John Knox, 2015.

———. "A Word for Trayvon." Trinity United Church of Christ, Chicago, July 14, 2013. https://www.youtube.com/watch?v=X7FhMwHi-lE.

Mote, Edward. "The Solid Rock." Public domain hymn, 1834.

Obama, Barack. "Second Inaugural Address." US presidential inauguration, Washington, DC, January 20, 2013.

Osmer, Richard R. *Practical Theology: An Introduction.* Grand Rapids, MI: Eerdmans, 2008.

Rauschenbusch, Walter. *Christianity and the Social Crisis.* New York: Macmillan, 1913.

Ray, Roger L. "Trayvon Is Dead and None of Us Are 'Not Guilty.'" The Emerging Church (formerly Community Christian Church), Springfield, Missouri, July 14, 2013. https://youtu.be/4BqDYwaMygA.

Rothman, Lily. "What Martin Luther King Really Thought About Riots." *Time,* April 28, 2015. https://time.com/3838515/baltimore-riots-language-unheard-quote/.

Simmons, Martha, and Frank A. Thomas, *In Preaching with Sacred Fire: An Anthology of African American Sermons, 1750–Present.* New York: Norton, 2010.

Sinibaldo, Geoff T. "On Barth, the Bible and the Newspaper." March 5, 2015. *sinibaldo.wordpress.com.* sinibaldo.wordpress.com/2015/03/05/on-barth-the-bible-and-the-newspaper/.

Thomas, Frank A. *How to Preach a Dangerous Sermon.* Nashville: Abingdon, 2018.

Thompson, Lisa L. *Preaching the Headlines: Possibilities and Pitfalls.* Minneapolis: Fortress Press, 2021.

Thurman, Howard. *Jesus and the Disinherited.* New York: Abingdon, 1949.

―――. *With Head and Heart: The Autobiography of Howard Thurman.* New York: Harcourt Brace, 1979.

Tisdale, Leonora Tubbs. *Prophetic Preaching: A Pastoral Approach.* Louisville, KY: Westminster John Knox, 2010.

Vrbicek, Benjamin. "When Should a Pastor Address a Current Event?" *For the Church* (blog), Midwestern Seminary, February 13, 2018. https://ftc.co/resource-library/blog-entries/when-should-a-pastor-address-a-current event.

Ward, James, and Christine Ward. *Preaching from the Prophets.* Nashville: Abingdon, 1995.

Wax, Trevin. "When Should a Church Address a Current Event?" *The Gospel Coalition* (blog), September 5, 2017. https://www.thegospelcoalition.org/blogs/trevin-wax/when-should-a-church-address-a-current event.

Weems, Renita J. "Scream." Riverside Church, New York City, February 20, 2015. https://www.youtube.com/watch?v=2gPB-w2XP5Y.

Wesley, Howard-John. "A Rizpah Response." Alfred Street Baptist Church, Alexandria, Virginia, March 25, 2012. https://www.youtube.com/watch?v=vkg2_pVfjMU.

―――. "Tell Your Own Story." Alfred Street Baptist Church, Alexandria, Virginia, November 8, 2015. http://www.alfredstreet.org/videos-on-demand/tell-your-own-story/.

―――. "When the Verdict Hurts." Alfred Street Baptist Church, Alexandria, Virginia, July 14, 2013. https://www.youtube.com/watch?v=hqhOe85_vA8.

West, Cornell. *Black Prophetic Fire.* Boston: Beacon Press, 2014.

Wright, Clarence E. "Hollering at God." Chosen 300 Ministries, Philadelphia, May 31, 2020.

―――. "I'm Mad and So Is God." Love Zion Baptist Church, Philadelphia, May 31, 2020.

————. "When God Talks Back." Love Zion Baptist Church, Philadelphia, July 14, 2013.

Wright, Jeremiah A. *Good News! Sermons of Hope for Today's Families*. Valley Forge, PA: Judson Press, 1995.

Wright, Richard. "The Ethics of Living Jim Crow." 1937. https://www.scarsdaleschools.k12.ny.us/cms/lib/NY01001205/Centricity/Domain/908/AT%20Ethics%20of%20Jim%20Crow.pdf.